D1248420

UN DEVELOPMENT AID
Criteria and Methods
of Evaluation

UNITED NATIONS INSTITUTE FOR TRAINING AND RESEARCH

UN DEVELOPMENT AID
Criteria and Methods
of Evaluation

A UNITAR Study
by William R. Leonard,
Béat Alexander Jenny
and Offia Nwali

ARNO PRESS

A Publishing and Library Service of The New York Times

New York   1971

1/24/72 Bu· Dart 9·00

CONTENTS

Chapter Three

PREFACE

The work of UNITAR in the field of evaluation of technical co-operation projects was originally suggested in a note of the Secretary-General in February 1964. In the note the Secretary-General said, "It is believed that the Institute could be of great assistance . . . in working out more adequate techniques for evaluating the efficiency and impact of United Nations field programmes . . . The subject is currently of major concern to the Economic and Social Council and the Administrative Committee on Co-ordination . . . "

Subsequently, the suggestion was elaborated and approved by the UNITAR Board of Trustees in September 1966. Special circumstances delayed the initiation of the present study until 1967, but in the meantime preliminary consultations were held and arrangements made with some of the United Nations agencies mainly concerned.

This study was already completed before the publication of the *Study of the Capacity of the United Nations Development System*. The group who prepared this UNITAR study, in particular William Leonard, also acted as consultants for the Capacity Study.

The present study is in two parts. The first part discusses the principal problems involved in the planning and management of development projects, stressing the critical importance of systematic planning. This in itself would go very far in producing objective bases for evaluation activities during the life of the project. The second part deals with some of the tools of analysis, adopted from modern management techniques, which, if used for discrimination and judgement, would provide the decision maker with a much more reliable information base than is now generally available.

The draft of the study has benefited from comments and suggestions by officials of several United Nations agencies and those of an international panel. The members included: Mr. John Adler, Associate Director, Programming and Budget Department, IBRD; Mr. Jagdish Bhagwati, Professor, Delhi University; Mr. R. G. Caranza, Former

7

Member of the United Nations Committee for Development Planning; Mr. Emilio Fernandez-Camus, Senior Economist, Economic and Social Development Division, Inter-American Development Bank; Mr. B. T. G. Chidzero, Acting Director, Commodities Division, United Nations Conference on Trade and Development; Dr. Dieter Danckwortt, Chief, Conference and Documentation Division, German Foundation for Developing Countries; and H. E. Mr. Aleksei Vasilyevich Zakharov, Ambassador Extraordinary and Plenipotentiary, Deputy Permanent Representative of the Union of Soviet Socialist Republics to the United Nations.

The Executive Director wishes to acknowledge most warmly the extensive support and co-operation UNITAR has received from the specialized agencies and other agencies operating within the general United Nations framework. Agencies of the United Nations system have been most generous in supplying research material requested of them, carrying on correspondence, participating in direct consultations and giving general support of the objectives of the study. Special mention should be made of the advice and support of a number of officers of the United Nations Development Programme. In addition, the Executive Director wishes to express his appreciation to the evaluation officers of several Governments for similar forms of assistance.

The study was prepared by William R. Leonard in association with Béat Alexander Jenny and Ofia Nwali. Mr. Leonard was for many years the Director of the Bureau of Technical Assistance Operations in the United Nations Secretariat, and before that the Director of the Statistical Office of the United Nations. His extensive experience in international technical co-operation and his professional competence are assurances of the quality and practicability of this study. The Institute is very appreciative of the time and effort which Mr. Leonard has contributed to this study.

The Institute as such takes no position on the matters studied under its auspices. It, however, assumes responsibility for determining whether a study merits publication and dissemination. The views, interpretations and conclusions in this study are those of the authors.

S. O. ADEBO
Executive Director

May 1970

PART I: PROBLEMS AND APPROACHES IN EVALUATION

INTRODUCTION

In recent years the governing bodies of almost all the members of the United Nations system of agencies concerned with economic and social development have expressed concern and have passed resolutions about the need for evaluation. Such actions have usually been initiated in the governing bodies by representatives of some of the principal contributors to the economic co-operation programmes. There is an insistence among these contributors that they and their legislative bodies need assurance that the resources made available are expended only for the most useful projects and for those which contribute directly, even though marginally, to the priority needs of developing countries.[1] In addition, developing countries have become increasingly aware of the need for systematic scrutiny of technical co-operation programmes in the light of their national objectives.

An impression prevails in some quarters that many of the technical co-operation projects are unrelated to national objectives and are products of indiscriminate selection processes. It is also said that projects tend to be self-perpetuating and that adequate scrutiny is not given to requests for continuation from one financial period to the next. To the extent that this is true, the problem may be ascribed to the pressures exerted by one or all of the participating parties or institutions, and perhaps in many cases to a kind of built-in inertia combined with the absence of critical appraisal of the project in terms of cost contrasted with the results achieved.

The doubts and unfavourable impressions about the merit of the programmes are, of course, only partially justified. The programmes have been useful, and in many cases outstandingly so. This fact has been amply documented over a period of years. The chronic shortage

9

of international resources in terms of mounting development aspirations and requests for assistance from all available sources, however, draws attention more sharply than ever to the need for carefully integrated planning of projects and for the critical scrutiny of results.

CHAPTER ONE

THE REQUIREMENTS OF THE SECOND DEVELOPMENT DECADE

While the impression of non-selectivity of programmes and projects has recently further stimulated demand for thorough and systematic evaluation efforts, probably the strongest incentive at present is the general recognition that the accomplishments of the first half of the Development Decade were very disappointing indeed, especially in some of the more important sectors such as agriculture. The General Assembly in 1961 set as an objective for the Decade "a minimum annual rate of growth of aggregate national income of 5 percent at the end of the Decade."[2] When the Economic and Social Council discussed the progress of the Decade in 1966, although adequate quantitative data were not and could not be available, it was quite clear that there was a substantial short-fall in expectations.[3] The Under-Secretary for Economic and Social Affairs reported as cause of the weaknesses of the development programme the fact that it "was still being treated in too general a fashion and that it did not have an 'operational significance' or specific content. It required a reference system which could be used as a yard-stick for measuring progress and within which preparations could gradually be made for joint undertakings covering a fixed period." This would need "a more convincing assessment of requirements" and "procedures for evaluating performance in relation to requirements . . . at an international as well as a country level."[4]

In the subsequent debate in the General Assembly, this general point was emphasized by the representative of the Netherlands when he said, "As the Netherlands Minister in charge of development aid had stated, the previous development policy [of the Decade] had lacked distinctive criteria as well as a quantified plan of action."[5] The General Assembly requested the Secretary-General to submit to it in 1968 (through the Economic and Social Council) "a preliminary framework of international development strategy for the 1970's within which initial efforts should be concentrated on the elaboration of specific goals and targets for individual sectors and components."[6]

While these goals and targets would not necessarily apply in all particulars to the development plans of individual countries, they would give an indication to all concerned of the sectoral composition and magnitude of the task to be accomplished if the aims of the Second Development Decade are to be met.

There is not necessarily a fundamental discrepancy between an international strategy for development and the development priorities of many if not most countries. This is implied in a statement of the Administrator of the United Nations Development Programme to the UNDP Governing Council at its fifth session that a "reasonably short list of basic fields could easily be established which would be acceptable to the requesting governments and serve as a well-defined and constant element in their programming procedures."[7] Food production, measures to control population growth, communications and health are examples.

Moreover, the requirements of national viability will in many instances strongly favour economic and other forms of co-operation among neighbouring states in geographical regions and sub-regions. Their priorities tend to correspond closely in such areas as free trade arrangements, industrial development facilities, multi-purpose river basin development, communications and transport facilities, meteorological services and certain types of training institutions. Where countries have a common interest in these fields, national priorities would probably not differ greatly from the priorities recognized by the goals of an international development strategy. This general point was taken up at the third session of the Committee for Development Planning in its discussion of the need for multi-national planning. In referring to sub-regional planning in Africa, the Committee noted "that effective multi-national planning may assist the smaller countries in their planning process, since the projects included in the subregional plan for agriculture, industry or transport would be taken over for implementation as national projects."[8]

Perhaps one of the most important effects of the "framework of international development strategy" to be prepared by the Secretary-General will be to draw attention again to the need for individual countries to review and strengthen, as necessary, their development plans and machinery. They will feel the need to establish a correspondence between their objectives as expressed in the plans and the financial and human resources estimated to be available from all sources for their fulfillment. Requirements may need to be assessed or reassessed and "procedures for evaluating performance in relation to requirements" established.

The problem of improved selectivity in order to concentrate scarce resources upon the most important development priorities was pointed out at the fifth session of the UNDP Governing Council in January 1968. In its report[9] it said: "It was widely recognized that, as the Administrator had pointed out, UNDP had, in a sense, come to the end of a first phase based largely on satisfying individual requests for assistance as they came in. The Governing Council was now more clearly than before confronted with questions of strategy, priorities and concentration. The several forms of assistance available should be applied in such combinations and sequence as to produce the optimum impact on the economic growth of the developing countries. What mattered was not only the volume of available resources—the supply side—but also and perhaps above all the quantitative and qualitative requirements of the developing countries for such assistance. The re-orientation of programming which appeared necessary called for a bold re-thinking of established patterns and the shedding of out-dated methods." Further, "It was pointed out that the Administrator was in fact emphasizing an axiom, in the sense that priorities had to be selected and resources concentrated on certain major fields of activity of primary importance which promised the greatest chance of success. The time had come for greater attempts to be made to reconcile national and international objectives and to integrate national efforts into regional and world-wide approaches."[10]

There is little doubt that the basic requirements are clear, and that the increased effectiveness of the programmes would go a long way to satisfy the generally recognized objectives. The objectives can be reached only by "a bold re-thinking of established patterns" combined with the creation of suitable international procedures for programming technical co-operation activities.

There exists, however, a number of institutional constraints, as will be shown later, which militate against the ability of the programmes to respond adequately to the priority needs of the governments. In addition, the fact that some 30 percent of the total development programme of the United Nations system is programmed outside the UNDP framework gives rise to other problems of management and co-ordination.

CHAPTER TWO

THE DIFFERENT ASPECTS OF EVALUATION

There is no longer any doubt that the process of evaluation should begin at the planning level before projects are formally initiated. It is at this point that programme decisions and financial commitments are made which may bind the parties concerned for a period of years. This is the point at which "evaluation," in the sense of *project preparation* (identification of needs), begins. The next stage is the *appraisal of requests* at which individual project proposals are examined to ascertain their relevance to the identified needs. Once approved, projects should be subject to *operational control* for the purpose of monitoring administrative and technical efficiency. Upon completion, projects are examined from the standpoint of an assessment of results to determine to what extent the projected targets were attained. Finally, an *overall evaluation of impact* of all activities of the United Nations system of agencies on national economic and social development may be made.

It is clear that some element of evaluation enters into each of the several phases in the life of a project. It is no longer adequate simply to conduct some kind of a post-project assessment of project performance on an *ad hoc* basis, for this does not produce evidence that the projects originally selected for implementation were the ones that contributed the most to the priority aims of the developing countries. Such examinations or inspections may indeed produce impressions or subjective views of how well the projects were operated and, hopefully, provide "lessons of experience" which may be used to guide future projects of the same kind. But this is not to answer the basic question of whether the projects were important and properly conceived or chosen in the first instance. *Post hoc* evaluations have a place in the system, and they can have clearly demonstrable value especially if the results can be tied back to the objectives and targets set out in the plans of operations. Even if this relationship can be established, it does not necessarily satisfy the requirement that project proposals should relate directly to priority components of the national plan.

It is important to emphasize, however, that many of the agencies within the United Nations system now are beginning to recognize that evaluation is a reassessment in depth of the economic, technical, institutional and management aspects of their operational activities.

CHAPTER THREE

PROBLEMS OF EVALUATION

As has been mentioned, Governments through the governing bodies of the agencies concerned have long been pressing for "evaluations," "critical reviews" and "assessments" of the results of development programmes. The basic legislation of the Expanded Programme of Technical Assistance[11] in establishing the Technical Assistance Committee, a standing Committee composed of members of the Economic and Social Council, instructed it "to make for the Council critical examinations of activities undertaken and results achieved under the expanded programme of technical assistance."[12] Subsequent legislation by the Council and other bodies reiterated the need for "evaluation" but without defining the term or suggesting methods.

A—Problems of Definition

In practice, the United Nations agencies have used the term "evaluation" in many different ways. The scrutiny of experts' reports is described as evaluation. The inspection of a project to determine its administrative or technical efficiency is evaluation. So is the narrative report of a visiting mission composed of outside experts. A descriptive report, without a trace of assessment, saying that two experts are in an East African country to advise on a particular subject is also referred to as evaluation. One United Nations agency insists that the term should be reserved "for those studies that permit a rigorous scientific measurement of the effects of a project." The Economic and Social Council refers to "the evaluation of the overall impact and effectiveness of the combined programmes of the United Nations system of organizations."[13] The *Ad Hoc* Committee of Experts to Examine the Finances of the United Nations and the Specialized Agencies used the following definition: "Overall [i.e., covering all aspects] evaluation consists in estimating the scope, cost and potential effectiveness of a project or programme before a decision is taken on it, checking the estimates and performance during its execution, and determining the cost and the results achieved when the project or programme is finally completed."[14] This list by no means exhausts the variety of uses of the term, which covers everything from pre-project review prior to approval to an assessment of results after the termination of the project.

In view of the confusion arising from the use and misuse of the term, the Inter-Agency Study Group on Evaluation[15] has recognized four stages of project activities, in each of which elements of evaluation enter, as follows:[16]

Project Preparation (identification of needs)

The processes by which the economic and social conditions and the objectives of development in a given country (or group of countries) are analysed, the specific needs for assistance are identified, the priority of the needs is determined and the consequent requests for assistance are formulated.

Appraisal

The processes the result of which provide a basis for decisions on requests for assistance in the light of established criteria, such as: relevance to the development objectives to be attained; propriety in terms of legislative and other requirements of the international system of development assistance; operational feasibility; and cost-benefit studies.

Operational Control

The processes, including inspection, reporting and other means, by which implementation of the project is monitored and reviewed in order to determine the extent to which it is fulfilling the stated targets and objectives and to introduce any necessary modifications at the right time.

Assessment of Results

The processes by which at an appropriate time before or after the termination of external assistance all aspects of a project are reviewed and the major direct and indirect results of the assistance are systematically determined and critically examined with respect both to the effectiveness of the project in attaining its objectives, within the context of the relevant economic and social objectives, and to the guidelines to be derived for the benefit of further activities.

The use of these terms and their definitions, as supplemented by related and subsidiary terms and definitions,[17] should greatly clarify the nature and meaning of evaluation activities.[18]

B—LACK OF SUITABLE NATIONAL MACHINERY

Fundamental to the process of evaluation is the fact that all development projects are co-operative in nature and are primarily within a governmental framework. The recipient Government has functions and responsibilities as well as the participating and executing agencies. This partnership has been fully understood from the beginning and has been stressed repeatedly by the Economic and Social Council. In 1963, for example, the Council "recognized that any evaluation of the impact is of primary concern to those countries [the recipients] and can be achieved only on the basis of systematic efforts at evaluation by the Governments of those countries."[19]

The shared, or perhaps divided, responsibility for programmes does indeed complicate the conduct of evaluation activities. Most Governments do not have evaluation machinery, so that any assistance they can provide is strictly of an *ad hoc* nature and the time of officials involved is taken from their normal duties. That the role of Governments in project execution is important is clearly shown in a study which has been conducted each year from 1956 to 1960 by the Technical Assistance Board of "major causes of results below expectation and of premature terminations." In forty-four countries studied in 1958,[20] on the basis of ten major causes of difficulty, it was shown that 70.5 percent of "occurrences" were attributable to the Governments. These difficulties arose from the lack of adequate administrative and technical services, lack of local staff or necessary equipment and the absence or inadequacy of counterpart personnel. (The problems involved in counterpart personnel, services and financial contributions still persist and are currently being examined to seek solutions.) Some 12 percent of the occurrences reported in the TAB study were attributable to failures of one kind and another on the part of the international experts. The balance was made up of miscellaneous causes, including inadequate pre-planning of projects.

In 1965, the Technical Assistance Board made a study of the extent to which recipient Governments carried out evaluations of Expanded Programme projects implemented in 1963-1964. Of seventy countries for which results were available, only 14 percent reported "systematic evaluation by co-ordinating authorities."[21] This meant that the national authority reviewed the status of all projects at regular intervals, although there was no evidence that specific methods of evaluation were applied. The procedure generally was that the projects were discussed by the co-ordinating authority, representatives of the participating organizations to the extent they were available, and the Resident Representative. In one country, discussions took place at the beginning of the project, mid-way in its progress and at the end shortly before the expert left. "Systematic evaluation," not otherwise defined, was carried on by individual ministries in 12 percent of the countries, and "occasional evaluation" by 19 percent. No evaluation was made by government departments in 55 percent of the seventy countries. It was found that in the relatively least developed countries, judgements could be expressed on the work of the experts but not on the success or failure of the projects as a whole.

It is obvious that national evaluation machinery should be intimately related both to planning and to executing activities. Evaluation, properly defined, begins with project selection and continues through the implementation stages of the selected projects. In commenting upon the first three overall evaluation missions requested by the Economic and Social Council, the Secretary-General noted the availability of technical assistance to advise Governments in planning suitable machinery for evaluation. Also, the Resident Representatives of UNDP and headquarters or regional officials of the multilateral agencies could assist in helping to establish evaluation procedures.[22]

C—PRACTICAL PROBLEMS

Frequent references are made to the fact that the totality of United Nations assistance for development is small in relation to national development expenditures and to bilateral assistance. To the extent that this is true, it is very difficult to distinguish that part of benefits derived which can be attributed to the United Nations programmes as a whole. This is particularly the case if the objective of the evaluation effort is that of assessing the "overall impact" of such assistance on economic and social development—the objective set forth by the Economic and Social Council. It is not really possible to do this in the sense implied by the Council resolution, because the actual situation is a very complicated one of joint costs and jointly achieved benefits. Any sorting out, particularly of benefits, with the object of showing what part of them resulted from United Nations assistance, would have to employ very arbitrary methods and assumptions.

Given the realities of the problem, evaluation procedures require to be applied at the project level. This was, in fact, the procedure essentially adopted in the "overall impact" missions. It involved problems of selecting projects to be examined in depth to the extent necessary to provide a basis for judgements. Many of these, in existing circumstances, were subjective, although in some cases it was possible to reach conclusions on the basis of objective data.

Even if evaluation is undertaken at the project level, the joint cost–joint benefit difficulty is not altogether avoided. All projects are supported to a greater or lesser extent by the recipient Governments, although in some cases the support provided, in practice, is nominal. On the other hand, government support of Special Fund projects is substantial. In 1967, for example, government counterpart expenditure was 1.45 times UNDP expenditure. For the duration of the programme (1959-1967), counterpart expenditures were 1.54 times those of UNDP.[23] Very much the same situation prevails in respect of World Food Program projects, although there is a much greater variation of percentage participation from project to project—WFP share of the projects ranging from around 10 percent to upwards of 60 percent.

In some cases, the projects would not have been undertaken at all had it not been for multilateral support; in other cases, the availability of external assistance provided the energizing element which permitted projects to be established. In still other cases, multilateral assistance allowed the addition of a supplementary and useful component to a prospective or on-going project otherwise financed.

It is not always easy, therefore, to apportion responsibility. Nor is it always easy to estimate benefits accruing from institution-building projects, such as technical institutes, educational projects and projects related to the development of economic and social infra-structure. The effectiveness of these projects will likely not be known for many years to come, and specific information concerning them would require special and rather detailed investigations in the future.

Evidence of the effectiveness of projects whch are essentially of an advisory nature is even more difficult to obtain. Most technical assistance projects are advisory and the results of many of these are intangible, not subject to any quantification or other objective outcome. They may, indeed, be strategic or catalytic, and thus success may be imputed.

This kind of situation constitutes "an essential dilemma in the future of technical assistance," according to an evaluation report by OECD on projects in southern Yugoslavia.[24] The report concludes that "the special contribution of technical assistance is to provide countries with help on those aspects of their development proposals that are frequently in danger of being overlooked, to advise on those actions that either do not get done at all, or else get done too early or too late, or perhaps inadequately."

Difficulties of the kind mentioned by no means imply that evaluation efforts are impossible or unrewarding. Deliberate and systematic project formulation can provide a degree of assurance to all concerned that United Nations programmes can produce benefits, even intangible ones, sufficient to justify their existence.

D—THE DIVERSE NATURE OF THE PROGRAMMES

The several governing bodies of the United Nations system have variously called for evaluation to be "systematic," "scientific" and "uniform." None of these concepts fits the elements of the development programmes as a whole, although one or all of them could apply to particular segments. The reason for this is three-fold. In the first place, practically every subject matter in the economic, social and cultural realm is represented in the programme by the operations of one or more of the United Nations agencies. The spectrum runs all the way from broadly general subjects, such as social development, to highly technical and scientific subjects, such as the use of isotopes in medical and agricultural research. No one formula for evaluation could reasonably apply to such a range of projects except in the most generalized way.

Secondly, the contents or constituent elements of projects are similarly very different from project to project. Projects may comprise single fellowships or expert advisers, seminars, training institutes, research laboratories, reforestation, malaria eradication teams, mineral exploration by means of airborne electronic equipment, the provision of food aid and a host of other implementing techniques taken singly or in various combination.

Finally, the size of projects varies from a short-term fellowship costing perhaps $2,500 to a multi-million dollar one dealing with planning urban renewal and development. There are more than 1,000 approved Special Fund projects, nearly 500 UNICEF-assisted projects operating, 300 approved World Food Program projects and several thousand technical assistance projects financed by UNDP and by the assessed budgets of several agencies.

Taking all these factors into account—the content of the programmes, the methodology employed, the wide variation in the size of individual projects and their number—it is clear that no single "scientific" method could apply uniformly. It will be necessary, therefore, to distinguish projects and types of projects to which, for evaluation purposes, differentiated methods and guidelines would be applicable.

E—THE QUESTION OF QUANTIFICATION

In a strict sense, the purpose of the evaluation exercise is to produce some kind of objective evidence of accomplishment in terms of outputs and to set this against the cost of the inputs, which in an ideal situation (seldom realized) would have been committed in the knowledge of alternative methods and costs of achieving the same or better results. This process implies a quantification of goals and targets against which progress may be measured and effectiveness evaluated. Considering the diversity of the development programmes, discussed above, quantification is no easy matter in many cases. At the same time it is suggested that so far, efforts to quantify have not been sufficiently assiduous or imaginative. Even in the absence of what might be called direct or specific indicators, there may well be indicators, one or two stages removed, which could reasonably be expected to be highly correlated with the more direct or specific ones, if they existed.

Even in cases where base-line data cannot reasonably be established at the time of approval of the project, there is in almost all cases a kind of intermediate position. This would consist of a detailed planning of work distinguishing specified steps or activities to be undertaken, each with an estimated completion time. This procedure would at least give indications of whether a project had been properly organized and implemented, even if it contributed little if anything to an assessment of results.

These points will be elaborated in part II of the study, which deals with specific methods of evaluation. They are only mentioned here in the context of difficulties encountered in establishing and using reasonably objective criteria in the processes of evaluation.

F—COST CONSIDERATIONS

Another practical problem, which has been discussed repeatedly, is that of cost, both to the operating agency and to the Government concerned. Any reasonably systematic work is likely to involve substantial cost, and it has been argued that a country is deprived of assistance by reason of project or agency money being spent on evaluation.

It is interesting to note, however, that in his Draft Programme and Budget for 1967-1968, the Director-General of UNESCO said: "I propose for the future to establish evaluation on a systematic basis, by making it an integral part of the work plan—and budget—of a project, from its start and throughout its duration."[25] This would not apply to all projects, but to the most typical ones. Resolution 3.02 of the fifteenth conference invited member states, inter alia "to participate in scientific evaluations in certain of the Organization's projects . . ."[26]

The Director-General of FAO, in his Programme of Work and Budget 1970-1971, says that "evaluation activities include responsibility for post-project and follow-up evaluation and for *ad hoc* evaluation during project implementation as a regular practice."

At its fifty-first (1967) session, the International Labour Conference said in its resolution on the Evaluation of Technical Co-operation Programme, after having cautioned against "devoting to evaluation resources out of proportion to [project] objectives," that "It would be useful to allocate part of the credits for selected projects to a more systematic evaluation of their objectives, their implementation and the results achieved."

The cost problem was summarized by OECD as follows: "Evaluation is not an academic but a purposeful exercise, a form of control designed to promote improvements and/or savings." By using methods that are as "scientific as possible, care must therefore be taken to make sure that the cost of evaluation and the resulting inevitable disturbance while checking operations do not outweigh the improvements and savings it may afford. In other words, the studies should include a cost benefit analysis of evaluation itself."

It is fortunate that the cost problem now seems to be placed in a perspective which recognizes the need for thorough initial appraisal and systematic monitoring. With attention turning more and more to identification of country needs and to the appraisal of requests, it is inevitable that costs of project preparation and operation will increase. To the extent that these activities are successful, the costs will be repaid more than amply. Unnecessary losses have occurred which might have been avoided through more careful planning and closer appraisal of national development programmes, with resulting benefit to the Governments, the agencies concerned and the programme as a whole.

It is to be considered whether or not a percentage of estimated project cost should not be specifically earmarked for expenses involved in project preparation and to the subsequent phases in the life of a project where elements of evaluation are present. The percentage might well vary from project to project, depending upon its probable complexity. On the other hand, in the interests of simplicity, a uniform percentage—say two or three percent—might be charged against each project and the consequent earmarkings pooled in a special account for use selectively as required.

Charges of this kind against the programme as a whole can be compared with research and development costs (R and D) which increasingly form a separate part of budgets and in some cases a conspicuously large part. Such a practice, applied to economic development, and financed by the international agencies, would most certainly seem justified. Judicious use of the R and D account would add a significant degree of certainty to the adequacy of project planning and execution, thereby avoiding possible mistakes in initial planning and in the operational stage. The R and D technique is a further example of the modern management approach which could be easily adapted to development programmes of the United Nations system. The cost of evaluation of a single project should not necessarily be judged in relation to its direct or immediate benefits. To do so would ignore possible long-term indirect benefits and improvements in planning and programming through the feedback effects.

G—THE OBJECTIVES OF EVALUATION

The following principles are proposed as Food and Agriculture Organization objectives:

(1) improving the selection and formulation of projects and programmes to suit the institutional framework and the development priorities of the recipient countries;

(2) identifying the interrelationships between projects for the purpose of evolving a coherent and effective country programme, with maximum impact on development;

(3) adapting the scope, objectives, strategy and design of on-going projects in the light of changing technical, economic and institutional conditions;

(4) suggesting measures for increasing the efficiency of project implementation and modification in project design that will enable rapid implementation;

(5) reviewing the technical, economic and social findings and recommendations of completed projects with a view to stimulating appropriate follow-up investment action with impact on development;

(6) improving the methodology of evaluation for future projects and programmes;

(7) drawing appropriate conclusions from the findings of project and programme evaluation for the purpose of improving the planning activities of the United Nations system and member Governments.

H—GLOSSARY OF TERMS USED IN THE EVALUATION OF ASSISTED DEVELOPMENT ACTIVITIES

The following is a first list of terms used in the evaluation of national or multinational economic and social development activities assisted by international organizations. It has been prepared in the context of the understanding that elements of evaluation enter to a greater or lesser extent into each phase of such an activity. The list is restricted to those terms which not only have special relevance to the evaluation processes but also require precise definition for the purposes of those processes. It intentionally excludes, therefore, those terms which, although relevant and widely used, are well understood, such as "advisory services," "experts," "equipment," etc.; "cost-benefit ratios," "multiplier effects," "impact," etc.; "joint projects," etc.

The glossary relates only to terms applicable to *project evaluation* and is not necessarily applicable to *programme evaluation,* which may be of a different character and subject to different methods. A study of programme evaluation will be taken up later.

The concept of evaluation may be related to four distinct phases in development assistance activities, in each of which elements of evaluation enter to a greater or lesser extent. These phases are: project preparation, appraisal of requests, operational control and assessment of results.

GLOSSARY OF TERMS

Project

An improved national or multinational development activity of varying complexity to which the Government or Governments and the participating international organization or organizations contribute specified inputs in order to attain defined objectives.

Experimental project

A project designed to investigate and test methods and techniques, under defined conditions, for possible wider application.

Pilot or demonstration project

A project designed to promote development through the demonstration, on a limited scale, of the applicability and effectiveness of certain tested methods and techniques.

Integrated development project

A project combining various elements of different economic and/or social sectors or sub-sectors in an organic relationship.

National project of regional development

A project designed to assist the integrated development of a particular region, zone or area within a country.

Regional project

A multinational development activity in which some or all of the countries of a particular geographical region participate.

Interregional project

A multinational development activity in which some or all of the countries of two or more geographical regions participate.

Project objectives

The stated purposes and aims of a particular project; to be distinguished from broadly defined development objectives.

Targets

A statement of the expected achievements at the different stages of a project.

Plan of operation

A formal agreement on a project between the Government(s) and the organization(s) concerned setting out the objectives, terms and conditions of the projects and respective responsibilities of each party to the agreement.

Plan of work

A detailed statement of the proposed organization of the activities of a project during each of its different stages.

Counterpart

Refers to government inputs to the project, which should be specified, for example, *counterpart financial contribution, counterpart services* or *counterpart personnel.*

Fellowship

Assistance to a Government to enable an individual to undertake specified study or training abroad for a period usually not less than three months. A fellow is to be distinguished from a *participant*, for whom financial assistance is provided to take part in a seminar, study group, study tour, workshop or similar activity.

Appraisal

The processes the results of which provide a basis for decisions on requests for assistance in the light of established criteria, such as: relevance to the development objectives to be attained; propriety in terms of legislative and other requirements of the international system of development assistance; operational feasibility; and cost-benefit studies.

Operational control

The processes, including methods of inspection, reporting and other means, by which implementation of the project is monitored and reviewed in order to determine the extent to which it is fulfilling the stated target and objectives and to introduce any necessary modifications at the right time.

Assessment of results

The processes by which, at an appropriate time before or after the termination of external assistance, all aspects of a project are reviewed and the major direct and indirect results are systematically determined and critically examined with respect both to the effectiveness of the project in attaining its objectives, within the context of the relevant economic and social objectives, and to the guidelines to be derived for the benefit of further activities.

Follow-up

Action taken by the appropriate institutions in a recipient country, with external assistance as and when required, in consequence of findings or recommendations of a project.

CHAPTER FOUR

THE SIZE AND COST OF THE PROGRAMMES

In efforts to evaluate the overall impact on economic and social development of United Nations-financed programmes, it has been said that "United Nations' aid is a small fraction of a small fraction."[27] This depends, of course, on what magnitudes are being compared. Is it small in relation to gross domestic product, to the total of bilateral assistance in technical co-operation, to the national development budget? It is difficult to generalize so broadly, because doing so may lead to the conclusion that such a small fraction is not worth bothering about and that United Nations activities are composed of low-priority projects which other financing agencies have rejected. Such views may lead to the further conclusion that it is not worthwhile to spend part of the resources for better programming and for systematic and factually-based evaluations.

From the standpoint of the international agencies themselves, evaluation of development activities would appear to be an indisputable requirement for effective programme management. In 1966 and 1967, some 52 percent of agency expenditures came from extra-budgetary sources; in 1968 it is estimated that 53 percent will come from these sources.[28] Funds thus received are almost wholly used for development purposes. These percentages do not include technical co-operation activities financed by the assessed budgets. If these are included, the amount spent for development would be in the neighbourhood of 60 percent.

Although United Nations programmes are relatively small, they are known to produce significant results in several ways. In some cases, programme expenditures dominate a sector or a sub-sector of the national economic and social programme. In other cases, United Nations programmes occupy a strategic position as far as progress in development is concerned by their catalytic or multiplier effect. In still other instances, advice from international sources may prevent a reckless and potentially disastrous commitment by a national Government. These results are on the credit side; on the debit side are known cases of dismal failures or, more frequently, of doubtful and inconclusive benefits. All these matters are of concern to the receiving Governments, to the international agencies involved and to the donor Governments.

The matter of smallness or relative smallness, however, impresses neither the various governing bodies concerned nor the donor Governments, particularly the larger ones. In general, appropriations for international aid are becoming harder and harder to obtain from the national legislative bodies. This applies equally to funds intended for multilateral programmes and for bilateral programmes. A number of donor countries are now taking a close look—some of them for the first time—at the results of their bilateral activities, as well as insisting that the multilateral agencies produce convincing evidence of the wisdom of their expenditures of contributed resources.

A—ELEMENTS OF TOTAL COST

The impression of smallness is supported by the fact that the international programmes are not consolidated for either financial or substantive programme scrutiny. Apart from the United Nations Development Programme proper, which indeed dominates the total effort, there are "regular" programmes of the participating and executing agencies supported by their assessed budgets,[29] other funds from various sources placed at their disposal, the World Food Program, the programmes of UNICEF, the High Commissioner for Refugees, the United Nations Relief and Works Agency, and activities financed by special trust funds, voluntarily contributed.

In the biennium 1965-1966, the field expenditures on behalf of UNDP Special Fund projects amounted to more than $400 million, including counterpart expenditures of the receiving Governments and an estimate of "associated assistance"[30] to the Special Fund projects. UNDP expenditures on technical assistance amounted to $101.4 million. The regular programmes of technical assistance of the participating and executing agencies came to $71.8 million, augmented to the extent of $31.6 million by the provision of associate experts and experts recruited on a payments basis.[31] Total technical assistance expenditure in the biennium was therefore $204.8 million, distributed about equally between the resources of UNDP and those of other agencies.

World Food Program expenditures were about $45 million (excluding emergency aid), and those of UNICEF, UNRWA and HCR together were about $100 million. The total field expenditure for development programmes in 1965-1966 was of the order of three quarters of a billion dollars.

This is a substantial sum; it does not, however, include elements for which exact figures or estimates are not available. These include: technical co-operation activities of the IBRD group and IMF; the direct administrative costs of all the agencies concerned (these were estimated in 1964 to be approximately 20 percent[32] of field programme expenditures, disregarding any part of agency general overhead costs); the counterpart expenditures of recipient Governments on the technical assistance programmes (these also amount to a substantial sum, even though there is a considerable short-fall in performance as compared with commitments); UNICEF estimates that $2.50 is received in contributions for every $1.00 spent from UNICEF funds; counterpart contributions to WFP projects in cash or kind; "associated assistance" to WFP projects from bilateral and other sources which over the life of the programme has amounted to at least several hundred thousand dollars; time spent on field assignments by staff members of the agencies when the cost is not borne by the field programme; "volunteer" personnel assigned to some agencies but not paid for by the agencies; and research costs for programme support by the regular establishments of the agencies. There is therefore a considerable part of total expenditure which does not reach the official financial accounts or published estimates. If only the most easily identifiable of these omissions are taken into account, this would bring expenditures from all sources for the biennium to well over a billion dollars.

B—TOTAL COSTS AND TOTAL PROGRAMMES

It would be greatly in the interests of total programme evaluation that systematic accounts, of a memorandum nature if nothing else, be maintained to record expenditures outside the assessed budgets and the pledged inter-governmental contributions to the operational programmes maintained by the United Nations family of agencies. In addition, agency accounts should distinguish operational expenditures in the field, direct programme administrative costs and costs of the headquarters establishment subdivided between operational and other. All expenditures for field operations, whatever the source of funds, should be broken down by sector and sub-sector.

An effort should also be made to prepare and maintain estimates of all contributed resources and services, expenditures for which do not reach the financial accounts of the administering international agency. These are now being recorded for "associated assistance" provided to Special Fund projects by a variety of donor Governments and institutions,[33] and for government counterpart expenditures.

Unless all the financial costs of all the programmes are recorded, it is not possible for Governments and programme managements to have a complete picture of resources and programmes. It is especially important in the light of the requirements of the second Development Decade, mentioned earlier, that the total programme of the United Nations family be subdivided by sector and sub-sector to permit aggregation by substantive types of activity as a guide for overall and sectoral planning.

C—RETROSPECTIVE DATA

In considering future programme development and possible read-justment, it would be very instructive to have available a compilation of past identifiable expenditures arranged by sector and sub-sector, ideally from the beginnings of the several programmes. Programmes of all agencies of the United Nations family should be included. This retrospective study should be based on a revised classification scheme. There would be a number of practical difficulties involved in such a study, because the basic information is widely scattered in the case of several agencies. A satisfactory series could be prepared starting, say, in 1960 with the advent of the Special Fund and increased contributions to the technical assistance component of the UNDP. The basic data should be on a country basis by sub-sector and agency. This array of data would permit an analysis of programme content over a period of time; it would illuminate the heterogeneous nature of the total programme, which is now more or less obscured by the vague and summary classifications commonly used.

It may be said that a fully satisfactory classification scheme by sector and sub-sector does not now exist. Classification schemes now in use are either too summary in form, or they refer too closely to organizational units which may have a diversity of operational and research programmes, or they are not comparable from programme to programme or have other shortcomings which greatly impair their usefulness for the purpose described above.[34] The preparation of a suitable scheme, designed for purposes of programme analysis, is an urgent requirement.[35] Such a revised classification scheme should take account of a possible future computerization of programme data.

The use of a standard system for overall programme review need not preclude the use by individual agencies of other classifications used for internal purposes or required by one or another of the agencies or by their governing bodies and committees.

The difficulties of preparing a useful and generally acceptable classification scheme are recognized. One specific problem concerns the classification of multi-purpose or multi-sector projects, of which there is an increasing number. This is a problem common to almost all economic classification systems; for example, the classification of industrial firms (enterprises) composed of several classes of plants (establishments) ranging from manufacturing to transport and construction is a persistent problem. In the case of the development programme, however, there appear to be a limited number of combinations, even on a sub-sector level. In order to avoid the allocation problem (by attributing the whole project to the major purpose—"the 50 percent rule"—or the difficulty of allocating to each relevant sub-sector the estimated costs incurred for each purpose), it would appear to be instructive to show the actual combinations, that is, a + c + d or b + c, separately as classification items.

D—THE CRITICAL FIGURE FOR PROGRAMMING

The figures given earlier all refer to expenditures in the biennium 1965-1966. From the standpoint of programme formulation and approval, however, they tend to understate the case. Special Fund expenditures or projects in the biennium, for example, were of the order of $135 million,[36] while commitments made in the period were about $184 million and Governing Council earmarkings (for the life of the projects approved during the period) were about $279 million, not including any government counterpart. The critical figure is therefore the earmarking, which in effect reserves the funds for each project. This is the point of decision. The same situation characterizes the World Food Program, where earmarkings for projects approved in any given year are considerably higher than the annual expenditures. Many other programmes are similar. The new programming procedure for the technical assistance component of UNDP, a form of "continuous" programming, provides that technical assistance projects may be approved for their duration although the funds are not earmarked in a formal sense. Individual country targets are established for a given programme year, say 1969, and apply provisionally for the next three years. Therefore, a commitment is made which may extend for four years but which involves annual allocations to the participating agencies. It is clear that forward earmarkings or commitments made in a given year and extending for a future period of years will considerably exceed actual expenditures in that given year or period. This emphasizes the need for the utmost care in programming.

CHAPTER FIVE

PROFILES OF THE TECHNICAL ASSISTANCE PROJECTS

A—THE LONGEVITY OF COUNTRY PROJECTS

Reference has been made to the fact that a great many technical assistance projects tended to continue from one programming period to the next, perhaps without too much scrutiny as to their suitability in terms of the priority needs of developing countries or the appropriateness of the methods used for their implementation. The stability of the programme in terms of content is confirmed by an analysis of a 15-country sample.[37] Table I shows that of the 367 sample projects programmed for the UNDP/TA component in the 1967-1968 biennium, with anticipated expenditures in 1967, 51 percent represented new projects and accounted for 46 percent of the value of projected expenditures of the programme in 1967. Projects started at least in 1965-1966 and continuing constituted 49 percent in terms of number of projects and 54 percent of 1967 value.[38]

There are two points of interest here. One is that the opportunity for new projects, reflecting new priorities or rearrangements of programme, is limited in each programming period by the continuation of projects originating in earlier years. Continuing projects are given priority in the sense that financial provision is made for them first. Longevity also means that very considerable costs will be involved over the period, a situation which should call for periodic scrutiny as to the continued usefulness and suitability of the projects. In the same way that Governments with economic and social development plans normal-

TABLE I
UNDP/TA 1967 programme[a] (Sample)
Experts' costs only
Number and value of projects in 1967 by duration
(Millions)

Duration	No.	Per-cent	Value 1967	Per-cent
Short-term—up to 9 months	67	18.3	$ 0.6	5.7
New projects in 1967–68 not continuing	99	26.9	3.3	32.4
New projects in 1967–68 continuing into next biennium or longer	21	5.7	0.8	8.1
Started in 1965–66 or before, continuing 1967–68[b]	141	38.4	4.3	42.6
Started in 1965–66 or before, continuing into next biennium or longer[b]	39	10.7	1.1	11.2
	367	100.0	$10.1	100.0

[a] As programmed. The delivered programme may be somewhat different.
[b] Fifty-eight of the 180 projects in these two categories started as early as 1956–1957; of these 27 started in 1953–1955.

ly review them in the context of the next financial period, development projects of the United Nations system should also be reviewed in the context of continued programme relevance and of financial capacity.

A further analysis[39] carrying the sample projects back to 1956 from 1966—an 11-year period—showed that 58 of the projects in the sample originated in 1956 and 1957 or earlier. In fact, 27 started in the period 1953-1955. In terms of value, 52 percent of total expenditures for the entire period 1956 to 1966 represented the cost of projects originating in 1956 and 1957 or earlier. If an allowance is made for the cost of long-term projects for which no expenditures were made for a year or two during the 11-year period (classified as among "intermittent" projects in table II below), the cost of long-term projects for the period would be 63 percent of total expenditures in the 11-year period.

Table III and figure 1 illustrate the same point. The declining percentage of the annual programme occupied by the long-term

TABLE II
UNDP/TA (Sample)[a]
Age and value of projects in the 1967–68 programme[b]
(Millions)

Projects

	No.	Per-cent	Value	Per-cent
Continuous from: 1956	30	10.3	$12.8	30.2
57	28	9.6	9.3	22.1
58	5	1.7	1.2	2.8
59	5	1.7	0.7	1.6
60	10	3.4	1.9	4.5
61	13	4.5	1.8	4.3
62	8	2.7	0.8	2.0
63	21	7.2	1.7	4.0
64	17	5.5	1.3	3.0
65	38	14.8	1.0	2.3
66	16	5.2	0.3	0.6
Intermittent[c]	96	33.1	9.6	22.7
	287[d]	100.0	$42.4	100.0

[a] Based on work-sheets especially provided by UNDP.
[b] In this case the value includes fellowships and equipment as well as the cost of experts.
[c] Projects classified as "intermittent" are those that were not continuous during the time period covered.
[d] The difference between 287 projects examined in some tables and the 367 in others is accounted for by the fact that the sources used for the latter tables subdivided some projects into parts which were aggregated in the other source.

projects results from the substantial growth of the technical assistance component from 1956 to 1966. It will be noted, however, that the value of the long-term projects in the sample, initiated at least in 1956 or 1957, tended also to increase during the period covered. Their value in the 1967-1968 programme ($4.4 million) was substantially maintained and even increased slightly over the preceding biennium, but occupied only 21.7 percent of the $20 million projected programme for the biennium. These values refer to the 15-country sample only and exclude regional projects.

It should be mentioned here that the definition of a "project" used by the different participating agencies and at different times is by no means uniform. What appears to be the same project over a period of years may have different components changing with the specialities of the experts assigned to it. For example, an agricultural project on "plant production and protection" may have a succession of experts such as those in desert locust control, cotton agronomy, horticulture and the like. Similarly, broadly labelled projects in "educational planning" may include specialists in rather diverse fields. Nevertheless, the above conclusions hold good for the broad economic or social sectors con-

TABLE III
UNDP/TA (Sample)[a]
Value of projects initiated at least in 1956 and 1957 which were programmed for 1967–68 and percent of annual programme committed to these
(Millions)

	Value	Percent
1956	$ 1.2	76.2
57	1.7	69.2
58	2.1	67.7
59	2.2	67.6
60	2.1	65.3
61	1.8	57.3
62	2.2	49.2
63	2.6	54.1
64	2.2	43.6
65	1.7	37.7
66	2.3	34.4
1956–66	22.1[b]	52.2
1967–68	4.4[c]	21.7

[a] Based on work-sheets especially provided by UNDP.
[b] Total expenditures (1956–1966) for projects in the sample was $42.4 million.
[c] Total 1967–1968 programme for projects in the sample was $20.0 million.

FIGURE 1.

Share of total programme expenditures for long-term projects starting in 1956 or earlier and included in 1967–68 UNDP/TA programme (Percent)

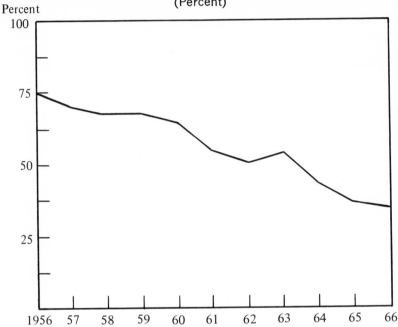

cerned, that is, for agriculture, industry and each of the seven other sectors recognized by the UNDP.[40]

While there may well be substantial reasons for such sustained efforts, for example in land use or cartographic surveys, it would appear that any project with an acquired or projected expenditure of, say, more than $250,000 should be a priority candidate for review and some kind of interim forecast of prospective results. It has been found in some reviews of on-going projects that results were far below expectations, so much so that the project was terminated or redesigned in order more effectively to meet its general objectives. While in principle every project should be examined periodically for this purpose, a pragmatic view of the situation suggests that there should be some initial selectivity with attention being paid first to the most expensive projects. Many agencies do examine or inspect projects on an *ad hoc* basis, but it could be argued that no project, particularly the large ones, should be continued more or less automatically without examination as to its effectiveness.

The new continuous programming procedure for the UNDP/TA component with what amounts to guarantees for life-of-the-project financing may result in even more stabilization of programme content if projects are planned for longer periods ahead, leaving even less financial resources for new and urgent requests. The advantage of the new system, however, is that it is designed to facilitate better initial planning by all parties concerned. It is supposed to reduce the temptation merely to extend on-going projects. Under the previous system of programming, there was some incentive for all parties concerned to fill up the target figure during the short programming period lest the earmarking be diverted elsewhere. Under the present system, the country target is guaranteed, so that there is no need for hastily prepared submissions merely to earmark the whole amount of the target. It is assumed that the new system will make it possible for recipient countries to take a new look at their technical assistance programmes so as to relate them more closely to their priorities.

An incidental benefit is the administrative one arising from the fact that a considerable amount of paper work will be eliminated. The former system required detailed submissions and approvals for each project every second year. The forward programme had to be projected anywhere from nine to 20 months ahead, and this resulted in numerous "programme changes" as countries' priorities changed or different internal and external factors came into play during the biennium. Each programme change had to go through the submission and approval routines. Programme changes also involved, in some cases, transfers between agencies if a country decided to switch part of its target earmarking from one major economic or social sector to another. This increased the amount of paper work, as both the loser and the gainer agency had to agree to the transfer through the machinery provided by the UNDP. Programme changes will not altogether be avoided under the new procedure, but more careful planning may minimize them.

B—THE SINGLE EXPERT PROJECT

An analysis of the sample projects, showing projects with one, two and three or more experts, confirms a generally held view that the "typical" project in the TA component consists of a single expert. Sixty-six percent of the 367 projects were so staffed, accounting for 38 percent of 1967 values. It is interesting, however, that the 67 projects (18 percent) with three or more experts account for 44 percent of the 1967 value, while the 12 percent of continuing projects so staffed represent 28 percent of value. (table IV)

These figures also suggest the protracted nature of many projects, but more particularly they draw attention to the large number of single expert projects. It is known that many such experts occupy the same assignments for five years or even more. Such cases would appear to be an indication of the need for an interim review of some kind such as has been suggested above for the expensive projects of long duration.

TABLE IV
UNDP/TA 1967 programme (Sample)
Experts' costs only (Millions)
Projects with one, two and three or more experts,
distinguishing duration of projects[a]

	No.	Per-cent	1967 Value	Per-cent
Single Experts				
Short-term	67	18.3	$ 0.6	5.7
1967–68 only	51	13.8	0.9	9.3
New 1967–68 and con-tinuing	10	2.7	0.2	1.6
Start 1965 or before and continuing	115	31.4	2.2	21.5
	243	66.2	3.9	38.1
Two Experts				
1967–68 only	25	6.8	0.8	7.4
New 1967–68 and con-tinuing	4	1.1	0.1	1.3
Start 1965 or before and continuing	28	7.6	0.9	9.2
	57	15.5	1.8	17.9
Three or More Experts				
1967–68 only	23	6.3	1.6	15.7
New 1967–68 and con-tinuing	7	1.9	0.5	5.2
Start 1965 or before and continuing	37	10.1	2.3	23.1
	67	18.3	4.4	44.0
	367	100.0	$10.1	100.0

[a] As programmed. The delivered programme may be somewhat different.

There are a number of reasons for protracted assignments, not all of them related to orderly and substantial pursuit of the established objectives. With a current *pro forma* expert cost of $23,100 per year for experts assigned to country projects, an assignment of several years' duration involves a considerable sum. In such cases a required interim review might support continuation, modification or termination.

C—THE TA PROGRAMME BY SECTORS

Table V shows the distribution of annual expenditures (1957-1966) by main sectors for projects in the 15-country sample. In recent years, expenditures for agricultural projects amounted to about 35 percent of total project value, having declined somewhat from 40 percent or more in the earlier years. In the period 1962-1966, other major sectors accounted for expenditures as follows:

Health	15+ percent
Public Administration and Other Services	13 "
Industry	12+ "
Education and Science	10 "

The foregoing figures, while probably reasonably representative of the UNDP/TA component, cannot be taken as characteristic of the development programme of the United Nations family as a whole or of the recipient countries. They do not include the Special Fund component, the regular programmes of the agencies (financed from the assessed budgets), special trust funds, the World Food Program, UNICEF and several other development activities of the United Nations family. The argument was made in the preceding section of this study that it would be useful to assemble the figures for all programmes, for a period of several years, on a more detailed classification of sectors and sub-sectors. This would permit a good many inferences to be drawn as to sectoral trends and the implications of these for future programme planning.

D—REGIONAL PROJECTS

Regional and inter-regional projects under the UNDP/TA component include (1) training institutes, (2) training courses, (3) regional and inter-regional advisers, (4) study groups, seminars, workshops, expert groups and the like. Training institutes are defined in this study as those which provide continuous instruction for six months or more. Training courses are of shorter duration, say from two to six weeks. Regional and inter-regional advisers are individual experts attached to the secretariats of the United Nations regional economic commissions and regional offices of other agencies who are available, at the request of countries, for missions of a few days or weeks and in some cases for several months. Study groups, seminars and the like are organized for short periods of time, normally not in excess of two weeks.

In the total UNDP/TA programme for 1967, regional and interregional projects represented a little over 17 percent of the $61.4 million approved programme, or $10.7 million.[41] Of this, $6.2 million

TABLE V
UNDP/TA (Sample)ᵃ
Distribution of expenditures by main economic and social sectors by years
1957–1966, in percentᵇ

	1957	1958	1959	1960	1961	1962	1963	1964	1965	1966
Agriculture	47.6	43.0	41.4	38.4	36.0	34.8	42.3	33.2	32.8	30.0
Industry	16.8	17.1	16.0	13.8	12.3	14.7	10.7	12.3	12.1	13.1
Public Utilities	5.4	6.5	9.3	9.4	7.8	9.2	6.6	5.5	5.4	6.7
Housing, Building and Physical Planning	1.1	1.3	1.7	2.7	2.6	2.6	0.8	2.2	3.5	2.1
Multi-Sector	2.2	3.5	2.1	2.6	2.5	2.4	2.0	3.7	4.6	5.1
Health	6.1	9.9	13.0	13.9	19.3	13.4	13.5	17.8	16.8	16.2
Education	5.3	5.5	4.3	5.6	6.3	7.8	7.6	10.5	10.6	13.8
Social Welfare	.0ᶜ	.0ᶜ	.0ᶜ	.0ᶜ	0.3	0.6	1.3	2.1	2.4	2.3
Public Administration and Other Services	15.4	13.0	11.9	13.5	12.7	14.2	15.1	12.6	11.8	10.8
	100.0	100.0	100.0	100.0	100.0	100.0	100.0	100.0	100.0	100.0

ᵃ Based on work-sheets especially provided by UNDP; regional projects excluded.
ᵇ Total expenditure $40.8 million. The difference between this figure and the $42.4 million in tables II and III arises from the fact that detailed 1956 data for one large agency were not available. This being the case, the figures in tables II and III on projects originating in 1956 may understate the number of long-term projects.
ᶜ Less than 0.1 percent.

was provided for experts, $4.1 million for fellowships and participants and $0.3 million for equipment and supplies. The two regions selected for detailed study accounted for just under 50 percent of the total expenditures programmed for regional projects.[42]

It will be noted that there is a heavy concentration of expenditure on regional and inter-regional advisers—nearly 62 percent. The use of these officers has tended to expand somewhat in recent years. This arrangement has proved to be a valuable instrument in meeting quickly urgent and unexpected needs of developing countries for advisory services. The ready availability of cadres of carefully selected experts located generally at the sites of regional offices avoids the difficulties and delays in the recruitment processes which in most cases would make it impossible for the agencies to respond to urgent and unpredictable requests for assistance. The number of advisers provided by UNDP is in some cases supplemented by advisers provided under the assessed budgets of the agencies.

The striking difference between the low proportion for fellows and participants in the sample regions compared with the other regions and inter-regional programme is accounted for by the fact that $2.8 million of the $3.4 million shown above is programmed for inter-regional projects. If this is taken account of, approximately $0.6 million is provided for fellowships in the other regions—Africa, Europe and the Middle East. This is close to the figure of $0.7 million for the Americas and Asia and the Far East.

The $2.8 million for "fellows and participants" in the inter-regional programme arises from the fact that some of the voluntary contributions to UNDP are made in national currencies which are not freely convertible, at least in part, to other currencies. The obvious course in this circumstance is for the agencies to organize short-term

TABLE VI
Distribution of experts in regional and inter-regional projects in the 1967 approved UNDP/TA programme by type of activities, number of projects, 1967 value and percent
(Millions)

	No.	Value	Percent
Training institutes	23	$0.7	10.8
Training courses	63	1.4	22.0
Regional advisers[a]	111	3.8	61.8
Seminars, etc.	50	0.3	5.4
	247	$6.2	100.0

[a] Including inter-regional advisers assigned to a region or sub-region.

TABLE VII

Distribution of the 1967 UNDP/TA approved regional and inter-regional programme by components—two regions

(Millions)

	Total	Experts		Fellows and participants		Equipment	
		Value	Per-cent	Value	Per-cent	Value	Per-cent
All regions	$10.7	$6.2	58.0	$4.1	38.3	$0.4	3.7
Americas and AFE	3.8	3.0	79.0	0.7	18.4	0.1	2.7
Other regions and Inter-regional	$ 6.9	$3.2	47.1	$3.4	50.0	$0.2	3.0

seminars and training courses, which they might well wish to organize in any case, in the countries where currency restrictions prevail. In the 1967 programme for inter-regional projects, approximately $1.7 million, or about 60 percent of the $2.8 million programmed for fellowships, were for participant expenses in connexion with seminars or organized in the light of currency restrictions.

The figure for fellowships normally reported under that heading included fellowships proposed for study or practical training in academic institutions, Government offices or installations, usually for several months or a year or two. It also included provisions for participants in short-term seminars, workshops and study tours. In the programmes of the two regions examined, $0.2 million of the $0.7 million recorded as proposed expenditures for fellowships, $0.5 million or about 70 percent refer to proposed expenditures for participants.

Experts assigned to regional projects in the two sample regions accounted for a projected expenditure of $3.0 million in 1967; of this amount, about 71 percent was for regional and inter-regional advisers. Nearly half (48 percent) of experts in the regions were so assigned. That they accounted for 71 percent of cost is explained by the fact that most of them were expected to be in the field for 12 months, whereas experts assigned to training courses and study groups normally spent only a few weeks or months. Typically, regional and inter-regional advisers are in the field on a variety of assignments for a period of years.

E—Note on the Sample

The sample used in the foregoing tables is that selected by UNDP for an analysis of sector expenditures for an 11-year period, based on projects programmed for the 1967-1968 technical assistance programme, showing total costs from 1956 to 1966 for each project. Fifteen countries and two regions were selected. The countries, chosen from each region and representing various stages of economic and social development, were as follows: Afghanistan, Algeria, Argentina, Central African Republic, Ceylon, Ethiopia, Iraq, Mexico, Nigeria, Pakistan, Philippines, Saudi Arabia, Trinidad and Tobago, United Arab Republic and Yugoslavia. The regions of the Americas and Asia and the Far East were chosen for regional analysis.

The total value of the 1967 approved programme was $61,420,-828. Fellowships and equipment were costed at $9,751,363, leaving $51,669,465 for experts. The cost of regional experts ($6,221,173) was deducted, giving a total of $45,448,292 for experts to be assigned to individual countries.

Numbers of experts, man-months provided for and the cost of the experts in the sample, related to numbers, man-months and costs in the total programme, show the following results:

	PROGRAMME	SAMPLE	PERCENT
Experts	2,831	655	23.1
Man-Months	26,381	5,775	21.9
Value 1967 (000)	$45,448	$10,134	22.3

The sample used in tables II, III and V has as a reference point projects for 1967 or 1968 or both years. Tables I, IV, VI and VII have as a reference point only projects with projected expenditures in 1967. See also footnote d to table II above.

The 15-country sample selected by UNDP was analysed also by broad economic and social sectors for the years 1965-1966. The results are shown in table VIII.

As will be seen from the table, comparisons of the percentages by sector between the 15-country sample and the total UNDP/TA programme for 1965-1966 correspond reasonably well. The largest absolute discrepancy is in agriculture, where the sample showed a higher figure than that for the programme as a whole. Industry, public utilities and education showed a reverse tendency. Some of these variations may result from the fact that different principles of classification may have been used in the two series. Such questions can naturally arise among the different sectors, as there may well be problems about how

TABLE VIII

Comparison of expenditures by sectors in 1965–66 of 15-country sample with the total UNDP/TA programme

(Millions)

	Sample		Programme[a]	
	Value	Percent	Value	Percent
Agriculture	$ 4.5	30.1	$ 24.1	23.8
Industry	1.6	10.4	13.4	13.2
Public Utilities	1.3	8.8	10.6	10.5
Housing	0.3	2.1	1.5	1.5
Multi-Sector	1.1	7.3	4.5	4.4
Health	2.4	15.6	16.2	16.0
Education and Science	2.0	12.6	15.6	15.4
Social Welfare	0.5	3.5	4.5	4.4
Public Administration	1.4	9.6	10.1	10.0
Undistributed[b]	—	—	0.9	0.9
	$15.1	100.0	$101.4	100.0

a DP/L.67, p.54.
b The sample does not include this category.

to classify agro-industrial projects such as those involving the processing of agricultural products. Such projects are difficult to classify because a judgement has to be made as to what proportions of the project mix justify classification as "multi-sector," or "agriculture," or "industry." Many projects have tangential effects on sectors other than the main one but would not normally be considered as applying other than to the main sector. Both series in the table include regional and inter-regional projects.

CHAPTER SIX

SOME PRE-CONDITIONS FOR PROGRAMME DEVELOPMENT

Substantial improvements in forward planning of programmes and projects would seem to require the existence of certain pre-conditions designed to assist in decision-making. The pre-conditions discussed in this section are mainly those under the general responsibility of the multilateral agencies and institutions, individually or collectively; others are mainly the responsibility of individual countries. These latter are discussed briefly in a subsequent section. In neither case are the suggestions made by any means exhaustive, but they do indicate possible avenues of exploration which may be useful in improved programme and project formulation, and actions which may be considered as contributing to more effective implementation.

A—INFORMATION NEEDS

Given the present institutional arrangements involving some 18 programming authorities, each with a number of sub-authorities, there is an inherent tendency for each to conduct programme discussions, at least initially, somewhat independently in the light of its own priorities and preoccupations. It is important that negotiations involving national officials, agency representatives and the Resident Representatives be held upon the basis of a common understanding as to (a) the basic economic and social situation in the country concerned as revealed by appropriate indicators, and (b) the sectoral development plans together with indications of financial requirements and the several sources from which these might be met.

Although in general national statistics in many developing countries are inadequate, especially as regards data oriented to development problems, almost all countries do compile certain basic data which can be used to illuminate, if not to define, the general level of conditions prevailing and their trends. The international agencies in recent years have given a very great impetus to the collection, improvement and standardization of the main categories of economic and social statistics. Many of these are available in the international publications, but it is suspected that they are not used in programme negotiations as systematically or consistently as they should be used ideally.

Almost all countries have development plans, although many of these are necessarily imprecise and others are highly theoretical. Countries do, however, need to have annual budgets or other periodic budgets which include anticipated expenditures for development projects in the public sectors. The expenditure plans should include both the capital budget for development and the recurring expenditures for such on-going development-oriented activities as education, health, agricultural extension and the like. Normal budgetary procedure also provides estimates of the origin and amount of resources expected in the same fiscal period for which expenditures are envisaged.

Systematic programme planning would involve study of statistical indicators, particularly those representing the main economic and social sectors,[43] together with study of the sectoral development plans—long-term and medium-term—as well as the development expenditure plans contained in the national budgets. Documents containing these figures could provide a common basis of information for programming discussions by the parties concerned. Availability of information of this kind could usefully guide discussions of new programme needs, as well as affording a recurrent basis for scrutinizing on-going programmes, especially those of long standing. The use of statistical indicators and planned sector expenditures in the process of programme preparation might assist in suggesting present and future bottlenecks in the total development effort, even though it would not be generally possible in present conditions to combine these and other relevant data in an articulated economic model. The collection and analysis of these data are prerequisite for systematic programme planning.

The availability of statistics and information of the kind indicated would invite much more research than is at present undertaken regarding programme and project proposals. Its use would not necessarily answer questions, but it would invite questions that needed to be asked, and answers attempted by all parties to the confrontation.

This material would also be very valuable in connexion with the projections to be made to guide international actions during the Second Development Decade. If "specific goals and targets for individual sectors and components" are to be elaborated, as requested by the General Assembly, there would need to be a roughly compatible body of information available at the country level.

It would appear very desirable that initiatives be taken by a central United Nations agency to compile and keep current data sheets containing a comparatively small number of basic economic and social indicators, as well as a summary by sectors of projected national expenditure plans for development, at least for the next financial period. The data sheets could be made available to the national planning and executing authorities, to the headquarters and regional and country representatives of the international development agencies and to the Resident Representatives. International machinery already exists for the collection of the information; the main task is to organize it along agreed lines and to make it available. A few agencies now use arrays of data concerning areas of their specialized interests; these could serve as very useful adjuncts to the more general economic and social data being discussed here. (See annex.)

B—CONSULTATIVE GROUPS

The preceding discussion on national and international resources committed to development purposes did not touch upon information concerning assistance made available by the bilateral donors. In some official quarters, this appears to be a delicate problem and not one to be dealt with at the international level or by international initiatives. At the same time, information about total resources is of the utmost importance in programme formulation. Surely knowledge of bilateral participation in development projects is not a secret in the recipient country; for that matter, such activities are, in most cases, well advertised in and by the donor countries. In fact, a great deal of information on bilateral assistance is already known to the UNDP Resident Representatives. Here again, the problem is simply one of organizing and making use of existing information at the critical times of programme formulation.

Developing countries would no doubt benefit by the systematic array of information on bilateral plans, and United Nations agencies would be much more confident of the suitability of new programme proposals.

In this connexion, mention should be made of the "Consultative Groups" organized by the World Bank. The first one was established in 1958, and by 1967, 10 such groups were active. Nineteen aid-giving countries have been associated with one or more of the groups, as has IMF and UNDP. Where appropriate, other international organizations also participate.[44] In a few instances, "consortia" have been organized, two by the World Bank and two by OECD. The consortia are somewhat similar to the consultative groups except that the aid-giving participants may provide some pledged amount of assistance.[45]

C—RESEARCH NEEDS

In addition to the needs for current statistics and information discussed above, much more basic research needs to be undertaken with respect to the content of programmes and the methods employed in implementation. Technical co-operation generally is expected to

effect a transfer of techniques and skills to the citizens of developing
countries. A great deal has been written in support of transferring
"know-how" and many examples have been given of successful implan-
tation. On the other hand, there is reason to doubt whether success has
been as conspicuous as is sometimes asserted.

One basic reason for shortcomings in achievement has been the
inevitable tendency of experts simply to transplant to developing
countries techniques and procedures used in developed countries.[46]
This has been done without regard to the conditions of life and work in
developing countries. Institutional, political and social arrangements
vary tremendously from country to country, and methods that succeed
in one may not be at all applicable in another. Are many developing
countries able now to absorb advanced engineering and industrial
techniques? Is a developed country's educational system to be applied
uncritically in a country just emerging into the modern world? Will the
peasant farmer in an agrarian society accept innovations applying to
crop management? Similar questions arise as regards virtually every
activity undertaken by the development programmes.

The operating agencies of the United Nations system are well
aware of these problems, and many have taken steps to modify or
adjust programmes to allow for the environmental factors found in
countries at different stages of development. This task is by no means
easy.

The need for fundamental research on development methods and
techniques is strongly emphasized by Little. He says: "It is my belief
that countries, donors and recipients alike, are pouring money into
economic development in desperate ignorance of how money is best
spent for that purpose."[47] Even if the economic planner knew all that
was necessary about the main indicators and their trends, Little says
that "he would still be at sea." He cannot say how much money should
be spent on health without knowing the effect both on population and
on productivity of the population: how much should be spent on
education, without knowing much more than he does of the effects of
general education on production: on agricultural extension, community
development, or co-operation, without knowing more about the probable effectiveness of such programmes: nor even on industrial development without knowing more about how easily advanced techniques can
be absorbed by unskilled people or adapted to suit their lower
skills.[48] This may mean that new techniques will have to be discovered and known techniques adapted to different sets of conditions in
cases where this has not been done. Little concludes that far too small
an amount of money is spent on research, particularly in the field of
social sciences where "the need for more knowledge is greatest . . . and
the research is least." Similarly, much more research needs to be
carried on with respect to subjects of interest to developing countries,

such as the use of certain materials and the development of methods of production for small markets.

Referring again to the fact that one main objective of the development programmes is the transfer of techniques and skills, it is not surprising that 37 percent of the Governing Council's earmarkings are for Special Fund projects in technical education and training.[49] In addition, 20 percent of earmarkings are for applied research projects, many of which have or are intended to have training components. Both of these categories consist of institution-building in a broad sense and are to be distinguished from individual fellowships made available through the several technical co-operation programmes. With such large percentages of the Special Fund programme devoted to education and training and to applied research, at least two general questions arise involving research in programme development.

In the first place, for what occupations is training most needed? Unfortunately, at this stage too few countries have been able to carry out manpower surveys. Such surveys could indicate the present man-power stock in each broad occupational grouping set against current needs, with projections for future years of the strength needed on the basis of forecast rates of development in the different sectors.[50] In the absence of manpower surveys with projections, it is hardly possible to guess how to organize the instruction—whether the emphasis should be on training for industry, for agriculture or for some other sector. There are instances in which the output of trained personnel over a period of years will be in excess of the requirements. The reverse situation also exists. Both of these are special cases referring to the absorptive capacity of countries where a miscalculation results in an imbalance between supply and demand for particular skills.

The question also arises as to whether multilateral funds have been spent on the "best" objective. There is, of course, the argument that any training, whether or not utilized in the specific area for which it was intended, will in the end contribute something to economic and social development. Nevertheless, systematic planning resulting in a reasonable matching of supply and demand would appear to be the wiser course to follow in programme development when the needs are urgent and the resources limited.[51]

The other question, closely related, is that of the level of training, and here the same general considerations apply. It is necessary to form a reasonably correct judgement as to whether, in a particular country and in a particular occupational category, training should aim at the top level or the middle level or some logical mixture of both. The history of the education and training programmes shows an imbalance in many cases between top and middle level training and between academic and technical training. It must certainly be assumed, as regards developing countries seeking to expand their agricultural and other resources, that there will have to be a very large increase in middle-level technicians—agricultural extension workers, teachers and paramedical personnel, for example. The fact that a great many developing countries are at present mainly agricultural with large and dispersed populations means that large corps of field personnel will be required to introduce more modern and productive methods to replace the traditional methods.

It is unfortunately true in some cases that although the training programmes appear well suited to future requirements, the results envisaged may not materialize. This happens because there is a tendency for prospective students to opt for higher-level training on general grounds of prestige; even some Governments have pushed for higher-level rather than for lower-level technical training in spite of probable needs. The result is an over-supply of top-level personnel, unable to find positions and unwilling to accept middle-level technical posts, and an under-supply of trained technical personnel in the face of what is expected to be an increasing demand for them. This is not to say that the kind of short-falls described represents a universal problem, but a problem does exist. Suitable research would guard against serious imbalances and offer some guarantee that the "best" results would be obtained in as many cases as possible.

In both of the problems described, concerning the levels and the choice of occupations for which training should be given, there is need for initial research aimed at determining the most probable requirements in the future. Research is especially important in view of the large amount of resources being used for education and training purposes.

Research may also be applied to the methodological problem of how best to communicate the results of applied research to the operations which the research was intended to benefit. In some cases, administrative and financial arrangements are such that it is difficult or impossible to provide enough field staff to transmit and supervise the application of research results. Even when this is not the case, the acceptance of innovations in some societies is far from easy in the first instance.

Problems may also arise when the support services of the multilateral agencies are withdrawn at the completion of projects. Will the acceptance level of innovations remain stable, increase or decline? Should specific incentive measures to encourage acceptance be built into particular projects on the assumption that the general incentive may be too vague to appeal to a significant number of people? If so, how are the special incentives to be supported on completion of the formal project to avoid reversion to the *status quo ante*?

Considerable research is in fact being carried on through field surveys designed to find out what methods of communication and retention prove most effective in given situations. This is being done with respect to functional literacy programmes, some agricultural programmes and several others. No final answers or solutions have been found, but the fact that the problems are becoming well recognized is of importance. It is also important that these problems should be considered, as far as possible, at the project planning stage. Approvals should be withheld until some reasonable hope of solving the connected problems of ensuring eventual absorption of training and of making certain that the results of applied research, often encouraging, can be communicated to and applied by large numbers of persons.

It may be inferred from the foregoing discussion that to an increasing extent, research should be essentially operation-oriented, that is, to particular types of projects and programmes. Basic academic research is essential, of course, as is laboratory and experiment station research. The ultimate objective, however, is the application of research findings to practical problems of development. This may require further experimentation and modification in the light of circumstances found in particular countries at particular times.

D—STORAGE AND RETRIEVAL OF INFORMATION

Another aspect of research deserving further exploration and development, and regarded as a pre-condition of more purposive programme formulation and management, is the retrieval of past experience. Past experience needs to be organically linked with current programme operation and scrutiny.

A systematic retrieval system is not only capable of recapturing past experience, but it also has obvious advantages for the management of on-going projects. This is true for strictly administrative purposes as well as for technical and substantive information and decisions.

On the operational side, it can record and reproduce all factors related to the programme or project. In programme management it is important to keep up to date on all matters which affect the administrative efficiency of the operation and the progress of implementation. It is important to know whether scheduled commitments are being met or not. These include all inputs to the project set out in the work plan, whether they are the responsibility of the operating agency or of the Government or of other authorities concerned. Delays in the introduction of agreed inputs can seriously impair operational efficiency. A current monitoring system may provide the information necessary for the appropriate authority to take the indicated remedial action. It can also alert the management of the project to administrative matters, for example such as giving notice of expiration of an expert's contract well in advance of the contract date, so that action can be taken for renewal of contract or for the recruitment of a new expert if this should be necessary. Information of this kind provides an important management tool, and the lack of it in many cases has caused delay and frustration in the orderly and efficient execution of the project.

In addition to the streamlining and control of strictly administrative procedures, a current information system, based on substantive reports from the field and other sources on technical problems of implementation, on newly discovered methods or on those proved not to be efficient in the circumstances existing in the country, will yield important information for the technical staff of the agency. Their consideration of the problem involved may result in some modification in the plan of work of an on-going project, perhaps a revised time-phasing or the substitution of revised methods or amended goals and targets. This kind of feedback procedure may often be of considerable value in ensuring an effective outcome of the project.

But past experience is at least as important. After 20 years, there are probably not very many wholly new problems, although techniques and procedures may have changed. At the same time, there is little doubt that the knowledge and comprehension of the management agencies have improved and that management tools have sharpened.

That a great deal of experience has been acquired may be inferred from the fact that in the first 15 years of the Expanded Programme, more than 30,000 experts served in the developing countries for a total of 32,000 man-years.[52] This does not include experts serving with the Special Fund or experts with the regular programmes of the agencies. But for the most part, the lessons of experience repose in the memories of programme managers, in project files, in the experience and reports of experts and in the minds of national officials. This situation has prompted the Administrator of UNDP to state that the agencies "have no memory." There is very little collated knowledge about the factors and conditions which make for success and those which make for failure.

The retrieval of information from all relevant sources, including technical recommendations of expert groups organized by the agencies and policy formulations prepared by the several governing bodies, is becoming recognized as an important and inescapable responsibility of the administering agencies to improve project planning and implementation.

One international agency has assembled all pertinent information on the important elements of programme development and management in a computerized system, and some other agencies are considering similar arrangements. One large bilateral agency is setting up a computer operation based on a comprehensive and integrated reporting system reaching from pre-project appraisal activities, through implementation, and to the final assessment of results.

The question of information storage and retrieval is already being studied more widely. The Computer Users Committee established by the Administrative Committee on Co-ordination is to be concerned with some immediate administrative problems, but ultimately is to look into such questions as how the combined computer needs of the United Nations agencies may best be met in the future.[53]

In addition, the UNDP Governing Council at its June 1968 session requested the Administrator to report on "the feasibility of setting up and operating a system of automatic data storage, processing and retrieval."[54] Subsequently, the Economic and Social Council at its forty-fifth session adopted a resolution expressing interest in the study to be prepared by the Administrator and requesting co-operation with the ACC and other bodies.[55]

The ECOSOC resolution emphasized "that the first principle of the storage, retrieval and dissemination of project information must be the rigorous selection of material that seems likely to be of future use."[56] This, indeed, is the central problem. One school of thought insists that practically all information should be stored against possible future retrieval. The other school insists, as does the Council, that a "rigorous" selection process should be followed. The argument revolves around the respective costs of inputs to the computer. Discriminating selection requires professional decisions as to what bits of information are likely to be of use in the future and would therefore qualify as inputs. Methods exist, however, for simplifying the on-going process once the initial substantive decisions have been made.

As in other research activities designed to improve forward planning, project management and the assessment of results, computer storage and retrieval, or other equivalent methods in some cases, will cost money, but in the long run will more than justify the expenditure. No business concern would rely for its financial and programme decisions on the memories and files of a constantly changing corps of officials.

E—MACHINERY FOR PROGRAMMING

As has been seen in previous sections, the basic source of weakness in the development programmes of the United Nations system lies in the processes involved in the formulation of country programmes and in project preparation. There are two reasons for inadequate programming. In the first place, too few countries are now equipped with effective planning staffs and with authoritative co-ordinating and administrative arrangements. Secondly, the programmes of the United Nations system are fragmented and dispersed among nearly a score of autonomous agencies, a situation which impedes an integrated approach to the problems of developing countries. National priorities may be distorted or ignored, with resources committed to objectives which may not be of the first importance for economic and social development in particular countries.

It is assumed as a basic premise that programmes should be country-based; that is, they should be directed to the development needs of each country and not formulated centrally. Each country is different in its economic, social and political characteristics, and the multi-national agencies are required to assist in preparing programmes and projects adapted to national problems, including those which are "marginal but decisive."[57]

There has been considerable discussion to the effect that a country programme financed by agencies of the United Nations system should form a "coherent whole." Presumably this means that there should be some kind of balance or integration among projects in the main economic and social sectors of the development programme. This surely is not a necessary condition. What is wanted is a rational and integrated country programme taking account of all sources of finance: the national Government, international and bilateral sources and the private sector. It is not a matter of concern that any one financing component of the total programme has to be balanced or coherent within itself.

It is considered that the possibility of more thoughtful and systematic programming has been considerably strengthened with the adoption of continuous programming for the technical assistance component of the UNDP. This means that projects may be established as and when needed and, in principle, can be financed for the life of the projects (assuming the availability of funds). This scheme avoids the former problem caused by the necessity for country programmes to be formulated in a short period of two or three months, one or two years in advance of their operational period. This procedure gave rise to undue haste in programming and to subsequent innumerable programme changes.

Thus projects under nearly all the programmes of the United Nations development system may be submitted when the needs arise. In a few other cases, financial regulations and administrative practices might have to be adjusted to facilitate continuous programming, but these would not appear to be insuperable obstacles.

F—NEW METHODS OF PROGRAMMING

In discussing "a new look at programming,"[58] the Administrator of UNDP suggested that "one very important way in which the more general outline of needs can be transformed into project requests is a system of joint programming activities between UNDP and each of the agencies participating in the Programme." This would be achieved through discussions at agency headquarters and with the planning departments of Governments. "Joint programming" of the kind described has been initiated in limited and informal ways, especially with reference to Special Fund projects. In the January 1969 submission to the Governing Council, for example, projects representing some 30 percent of earmarkings were jointly prepared by various combinations of officials from UNDP and the executing agencies.

In another approach to the programming problem, the United Nations Department of Economic and Social Affairs undertook programme planning missions in two countries in 1968 and made arrangements for a third mission to be organized in 1969. The missions were carried out in consultation with UNDP and some of the larger agencies. The Resident Representative played an important role. The missions represented a first attempt at a systematic review of programme requirements in the light of the priorities of the national development plans and the prospective resources to give effect to the plans. The missions were experimental in a sense, but they may suggest a method which may be further pursued.

Another arrangement also being discussed involves the formation of sub-regional adviser teams skilled in the various disciplines necessary for economic and social planning. Each team, supported by the required background research by their headquarters, the regional commissions, development banks and institutes, could provide systematic planning services for several or a number of countries, as well as development planning and information units at their respective headquarters. Here again, financial and other considerations would imply a modest and experimental start in sub-regions most in need of assistance.

A much more far-reaching proposal, bearing on programming, was made by Max F. Millikan, member of the UN Committee for Development Planning.[59] Millikan suggests a World Development Council (1) to establish internationally agreed criteria for evaluating the national interest in the plans of both developed and developing countries; (2) to review the long-run plans of individual developed and developing countries in order to test their consistency with whatever global targets have been established; (3) to report regularly to the United Nations and the international public on progress under plans, and plan implementation; (4) to recommend periodically to both aid recipients and aid donors appropriate measures to accelerate development and to improve plan implementation. Although this is not a direct approach to programming, it is very closely linked in that a review of national plans and measures ("evaluation," in Mr. Millikan's terms) to accelerate development would be bound to have a very considerable impact on programme and project formulation.[60]

Such a World Council, however, seems very much in the future, meritorious as the scheme may seem in principle. As has been made clear in earlier parts of this study, there are 18 largely autonomous programming agencies. It is true that the agencies collaborate in a number of inter-disciplinary projects, or sub-contract a part of a

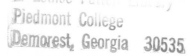

multi-purpose project. But this is not programming in the sense intended here.

G—PRACTICAL STEPS

Given the present institutional arrangements, what steps may be envisaged in the near term to rationalize programme and project formulation? It would appear that the solution must be pragmatic, empirical and selective.

A series of tripartite and multipartite programming missions could be organized on an *ad hoc* basis to assist countries to review the present complement of projects and to consider new ones. The missions would be composed of UNDP (including the Resident Representatives), the national planning officials, economic development planners, agricultural development planners and social development planners. The continuous programming procedure, now more generally used, would facilitate the conduct of the missions, since they could be spread out over time, hopefully to coincide with the periods of national plans and preparation.

Not all countries need be covered. Countries with effective planning and administrative establishments could be excused from the exercise, at least for the initial round. Missions to countries with very small programmes might have low priority. Larger countries, or those most in need of programming assistance, should receive priority attention. In any case, programme missions would not usually be required more than once in a two-year period, but it would appear desirable that they take place periodically. With such a selective approach, costs need not be excessive, having in mind that quite a lot of travel money and secretariat time is now being spent on missions despatched by the individual agencies.

An adequate information base would be needed to facilitate a systematic programme review. Relevant economic and social indicators should be available with some trend analysis. Particulars of the national development plans for the short term, intermediate and long term should be accessible together with data on the probable sources of finance, including a projection of what financing the United Nations system might be able to contribute, say in the next two years. National expenditure estimates should include projected capital cost, associated operational costs and the part of the current operating budget related to expenditure for education, agriculture and such other sectors as are related to development. An opportunity would thus be given also for the review of the main on-going projects to see whether revisions or other actions were called for.[61]

It is to be hoped that what might be called the institutional scope of the *ad hoc* missions would be broad enough to include the development programmes of agencies of the United Nations system not subject to review of the UNDP Governing Council. It should also include the regular (assessed budget) programmes of the agencies and special trust funds established for specific development purposes. As has been shown, these types of programmes together account for at least 30 percent of the total development effort of the United Nations system.

Whatever form of machinery may ultimately emerge from a consideration of the several mechanisms for the rational organization of programming now being studied, it is necessary, without question, for a start to be made. With programming operations strengthened and project preparation systematically organized, an indirect benefit would very likely be a rationalization of the heterogeneous and unstructured activities now carried on in the name of evaluation. Pressure would begin to be applied at the most vulnerable points. A sound programme with properly prepared projects will have built-in machinery for monitoring during the operational phases, with some basis to evaluate effectiveness at the end, and for feedback information to assist in future planning. Evaluation and appraisal efforts at the initial stage would produce important qualitative improvements in programme. Costs would probably not be more than the opportunity costs of poor projects, costs of projects that have to be terminated and costs of many *ex post* evaluation activities of various kinds.

H—ANNEX: A LIST OF ECONOMIC AND SOCIAL INDICATORS

1. Gross domestic product, per capita (period).*
2. Rate of change in gross domestic product (period).
3. Industrial origin of gross domestic product at factor cost (period).
4. Population by age and sex: 15-49, 50 and over (or more detailed).
5. Percent of labour force in agriculture, or percent dependent on agriculture (latest census or sample).
6. Percent of population 15 years and over unable to read and write (two censuses).
7. Percent of population aged 5-14 and 15-19 enrolled in primary and secondary levels (two censuses).
8. Birth rate (period).
9. Infant mortality (period).
10. Index numbers of agricultural production, total and of which food (period).
11. Exports and imports of food (period) and net balance, distinguishing currency areas if possible.
12. Other merchandise trade balances by major groups of the Standard International Trade Classification (period).
13. Terms of trade (period).
14. Government development budget: total, and of which education,

health, social services, public works, agriculture, etc. (this should be as detailed as possible).

15. Net balance of government expenditures and receipts (period).

16. Public debt, distinguishing domestic and foreign with projected debt service obligations for the latter projections.

CHAPTER SEVEN

PLANNING AT THE COUNTRY LEVEL

It is the professed intention of multilateral development agencies to associate their field activities as closely as possible with national development plans and the priorities contained in them. Realization of this intention, however, depends heavily upon the existence of plans, the efficiency of their formulation and the effectiveness of their implementation.

It is true that almost all developing countries have national economic and social development plans. These plans vary enormously in precision of formulation, scope and "implementability." They may be little more than shopping lists, described by Waterston as the "project-by-project" approach, where proposed public investment projects in mixed economies "are little related to each other or to a unifying concept."[62] At the other end of the scale are those countries which can prepare and implement comprehensive planning schemes, composed of "an integrated public investment plan and a plan for the private sector which have been reconciled with each other and with the overall targets."[63] Such schemes are based upon elaborate growth models which take account of all the relevant economic variables. Very few countries at present have the capability to formulate and give effect to comprehensive plans, despite the prolonged efforts by individual Governments and international institutions; this is exemplified by the experience of many Latin American countries.

There are important reasons for the inability, up to now, of a great many Governments to go very far either in preparing an integrated public investment scheme or in creating and maintaining a comprehensive plan. These reasons are cogently elaborated by Waterston[64] and in the report of the second session of the United Nations Committee for Development Planning.[65] Although the Committee at this session dealt mainly with problems of planning in Latin America, experience has shown that the difficulties found there have also arisen elsewhere.

A—SHORTCOMINGS OF MANY DEVELOPMENT PLANS

Deficiencies in the public administration, caused by political and institutional factors, mean that the status of the planning office within the Government is not sufficiently clear as regards its relationship to the executive or to the policy-making authority. There is a considerable body of opinion holding the view that the planning machinery should be administratively separate from the decision maker; that is, the planning agency should not be involved in the ministerial decisions required for execution of the sectoral plans. However this may be, a need exists for orderly co-ordination, and for the feedback of information from the executing agency to the planning agency. This suggests the need for the creation of effective evaluation and control arrangements which themselves will help to integrate planning and administration.

Moreover, many plans do not contain a satisfactory development strategy; that is, an orderly interaction of ends and means which takes account of broad economic and social aims and of capabilities for reaching them. A plan in the acceptable sense of the term is not merely a collection of projects; projects should relate to one another in a realistic way so as to achieve the necessary balance and relationship among the several sectors. A development strategy should also take account of the general long-term objectives sought, such as employment, income redistribution, education and other economic and social aims.

Many plans also lack operational components and machinery to transform elements of the plans into specific activities falling within particular sectors and tied to the periodic national budgets. Medium and long-term plans need to be reviewed annually in connexion with preparations for the next financial period. Conditions may have changed, there may have been short-falls in project implementation, urgent new or revised priorities may have emerged and exogenous factors, also unforeseen, may have seriously altered the premises upon which the plan is based. Here again, the importance of two-way feedback arrangements between planners and executors must be stressed.

The absence of timely statistics (and in some cases the almost complete lack of statistics) needed for plan formulation and implementation is a serious problem. Data are needed to record the position of individual sectors and the relationships among them. It has even been suggested that some of the financial resources marked for development be used to improve the scope and timeliness of statistics related to development and to restructure the statistical system if this should be indicated. The statistics should be oriented toward development problems, as these are the main tasks in hand.[66]

In this connexion, the lack of broadly based research on resources, techniques, bottlenecks to development and similar factors create difficulties in sorting out the crucial priorities to be satisfied by the scarce means available.

The general situation is very much the same in Africa as in Latin

America. Changes in government policies leading to successful implementation of development plans have not been made. Too frequently, unforeseen events, such as those arising from external trade problems and uncertainties attached to external financial assistance, have interfered with the orderly carrying out of the plan. Moreover, the necessary reforms of the administrative machinery have not yet been made.[67]

It also appears true that although existing statistics and other information are far from adequate, enough exists in several African countries to lead to substantial improvements in project formulation and execution. However, this information has not been taken account of at the decision-making levels. Few means exist, at the operational stage, to feedback important information to the planning levels of Governments. Even if essential data are available at the project planning stage in the current sectoral situation, reliable estimates of the probable resource availabilities and the constraints attaching to them are not sufficiently allowed for because of the lack of a fully organized information system. Whereas one side of the development plan–resource allocation equation may be at least generally known, far too little is known about the other side.[68]

B—THE NEED TO STRENGTHEN PLANNING MACHINERY

Given the difficulties that countries encounter in the preparation of plans and their implementation, it is not surprising that technical co-operation extended by multilateral and bilateral agencies may not correspond too well with the real priority needs of recipients. The assistance offered and taken may reflect the aspirations and motives of the donor agency, and in this way well-intended aid may be dissipated in undertakings which are of marginal value at best.

The Committee for Development Planning recognized the double problem of possibly immature development plans and the realistic programming of a technical cooperation in one of its recommendations. It stated that there is a need for "stronger technical assistance support and more effective utilization by Governments of the technical assistance for planning provided through international agencies and the institutions maintained by them; in that respect, Governments and agencies should be guided in the formulation and implementation of technical assistance programmes by the Committee's recommendations on planning and plan implementation. Also important is the co-ordination between the international agencies providing technical assistance for planning and the international financial agencies, in addition to the internal co-ordination between the various agencies."[69]

This recommendation was based on the observation by a member of the Committee that "Every country should therefore draw up a technical assistance programme as an integral part of its development plan. Only then should it apply to the donor countries for the assistance it required. Unfortunately, the developing countries did not have such plans; they should be helped to prepare them so that in asking for technical assistance they would know exactly what they were doing, and would be able to turn the services provided to the best possible account."[70]

The Economic and Social Council has for some time emphasized the need for developing countries to strengthen their planning machinery, in regard to both the substance of the plans themselves and to matters of administration and co-ordination, so as to facilitate practical implementation. As is indicated above, reforms of the kind needed will not be easy to effect in the face of strongly entrenched institutional and social factors and, in many of the newer countries, a degree of administrative inexperience. Moreover, the statistical and other research materials in most countries must be expanded and re-directed in order to adapt them specifically to development objectives.

In 1965, the Council requested the Secretary-General, the regional economic commissions and the specialized agencies "to continue and intensify their activities with respect to economic planning and projections and to the transfer of knowledge on those subjects, with the co-operation of the Governments concerned."[71] In 1966, the Council expressed the hope that the newly established Committee for Development Planning would intensify its work on planning with a view "to enabling the organizations of the United Nations family to provide technical assistance to the developing countries in the preparation of suitable planning methods and in the application of their development plans."[72]

In somewhat stronger language, the Council in 1967 invited the Governments of the developing countries to consider, "in the light of the recommendations made by the Committee for Development Planning and in accordance with the circumstances prevailing in their countries, the advisability of formulating concerted and vigorous development policies so as to bring about rapid improvements in mobilizing resources, in strengthening the machinery for plan formulation and plan implementation, and in initiating institutional changes which are essential for accelerating the process of economic development."[73]

In view of the crucial role of Governments in plannning, administration and co-ordination of development activities, and, in the case of a number of newly independent countries, an apparently excessive mobility of administrative officers, it would seem an urgent matter that the United Nations system find practical ways and means to provide substantial assistance to strengthen the capability of requesting Governments for purposes of development planning. Highest priority should therefore be given to training officials in the planning and management of technical co-operation.

C—THE NEED FOR RESEARCH

A number of countries in recent years have obtained international technical assistance in the preparation of development plans. It appears, however, that much more should be done, especially in the light of the probable requirements of the Second Development Decade referred to above. There is a need for a systematic analysis of existing plans in the light of known economic and social indicators. There is need for an appraisal of the causes of the existing gap between the plans and the operational activities designed to transform them into action. On the basis of this analysis and appraisal, the international institutions involved could invite selected Governments to request assistance on either the substantive level or the administrative level, or both. Having said this, it would of course be necessary that the Governments themselves take initiatives to commit resources in money and manpower for plan development. It would also be necessary for them to take decisions as regards administrative and institutional arrangements that up to now have constituted serious constraints in effective plan formulation and management.

Research is needed on the existing relationship between national priorities and the assistance given by the United Nations agencies. Empirical studies might be made of selected countries comparing the order of priority assigned to a sector or sub-sector, together with the financial provision made in the national development budget, with the rank order and amount of United Nations agency expenditures for the same sectors and sub-sectors.

An example might clarify this point. In one country for which this comparison was made, the top priority of the Government in terms of budgetary allocation (nearly one third of the development budget) was in sector (X), where United Nations expenditures were 8 percent of the country programme target. In Sector (Y), where the United Nations expended 25 percent of its resources, the country had allocated 2 percent. In sector (Y), national production was very small and the export value almost negligible, and any hopes for an increase very small indeed. As regards sector (X), its exports accounted for two thirds of total exports in a country where total merchandise trade was running against it by a ratio of 3 to 2. This would seem to indicate that the country was counting on development in sector (X) to provide means of paying for the imports of sector (Y) goods, where the balance of trade was about 20 to 1 against it.

This clearly raises the question of whether United Nations resources are being applied in the most productive way in the light of the priorities expressed in the national development budget. There may have been good reasons that governed United Nations allocations, but they do not emerge from this rather superficial comparison. In the present case it might be argued that some bilateral agency was looking after sector (X) in co-operation with the Government and that no additional assistance was needed. Perhaps, also, the private sector was involved to some extent. At the same time, such an exercise might well precede decisions of the Government and the United Nations agencies upon new programme proposals to minimize possible un-economic application of resources. At the minimum, this kind of analysis would raise questions which might easily lead to a more thoughtful approach to programme formulation.

If the plan is the basic instrument for development (although in some exceptional instances this has proved not to be the case), it is surely important that national resources be mobilized in systematic and purposive ways and that national energies be seriously dedicated to plan fulfillment. It is only in this way that the financial resources of the multilateral agencies can be wisely allocated among competing interests. It is only in this way that convincing evaluations can be made which will persuade the governing bodies of the agencies and the donor Governments that international assistance is in fact achieving the "best," or at least the "second best" results in efforts to reconcile ends and means.

In spite of the known weakness of strictly defined development plans, the Economic and Social Council and other governing bodies of the technical co-operation programmes have consistently advised Governments and the international agencies to link technical co-operation with national plans and priorities. Thus in 1958 the Council, referring to the country programming procedure adopted in 1954 for the Expanded Programme of Technical Assistance (in place of the pre-existing system of "agency shares"), requested Governments in submitting their country programmes "to make clear as far as possible to the Technical Assistance Board and the participating organizations, in the case of each project, its relationship to any general development plan or programme," its duration, objectives and relationship to any other similar or complementary project undertaken or requested under another existing technical assistance programme.[74] Similarly, it is stated in the guiding principles and criteria of the Special Fund that "due consideration shall be given to the arrangements made for the integration of projects into national development programmes. . . ."[75]

The Administrative Committee on Co-ordination, in commenting upon the reports of special evaluation missions sent to three developing countries[76] under ECOSOC resolutions 1042 (XXXVII) and 1151 (XLI), strongly urged that attention be paid to the priority needs of countries as expressed in their development plans. This view was subsequently endorsed by the Economic and Social Council.

The terms of reference of the special evaluation missions now provide specific guidance on the matter. "One of the key points is the development plans of a country. It would be useful to examine what contribution the United Nations system of organizations has made in assisting the formulation and implementation of the overall development plans and the sectoral development programmes."[77]

CHAPTER EIGHT

PROGRAMME PLANNING CONSTRAINTS

A—INSTITUTIONAL FACTORS

Mention has been made of institutional constraints which severely limit the flexibility of the programmes in response to changing conditions in the developing countries and reduce the possibility of resource consolidation in a limited number of strategic areas of activity. The constraints arise because there are 13 programming agencies, apart from the UNDP itself, and four other agencies outside the UNDP system with programmes related to economic and social development. Within most of the agencies there are several major divisions representing different fields of interest. These units taken together represent the priority programmes of the international system. This means that the numerous operational programmes are highly competitive among themselves, each programme being supported by the broad constitutional provisions of the agencies and resolutions of their governing bodies. Recipient Governments are therefore confronted with formidable shopping lists, the lists being conditioned by the financial constraints discussed below.

As regards priorities, Little and Clifford, referring to the Expanded Programme of Technical Assistance, noted that "their [the specialized agencies and the United Nations] official function, for which they were set up, is to promote international co-operation and research in their own specialized fields. This demands a set of priorities different from those needed for programmes designed for maximum economic development in particular countries and in particular areas [of activity]."[78] Galbraith also referred to the varied nature of the international programme in saying: "A hundred years ago the development of the trans-Mississippi plains in the United States called, above all else, for a land policy which would get the land settled and plowed and a transportation system which would get the products to market. To this end the Government surveyed the land, gave 160 acres to anyone who had proved his good intentions by farming it for a few months, and subsidized the building of railways. These essentials being provided, development proceeded with unexampled speed. It was our unquestioned good fortune that community education experts, grain marketing analysts, home economists, vocational counselors, communications specialists, or public safety advisers had not been invented. Had these existed, attention would have been drawn from the strategically central tasks of getting the farms settled and the railways built. And they would have been a burden on the backs of people who could not yet afford such luxuries."[79]

This institutional constraint finds practical expression in financial arrangements that have characterized the Expanded Programme from the beginning. In the early years, the resources of the programme were divided into "agency shares"; this resulted in a fairly stable percentage level from year to year. In fact, the initial allocation of resources was governed by a provision[80] in the basic legislation which assigned percentage participation in the first $17 million received to the then six participating agencies on the following scale: 29, 23, 22, 14, 11 and 1. In 1954, the Economic and Social Council adopted a system of "country programming" or "country targets," under which agency allocations were not essentially pre-determined as before but resulted from the summation of country requests in the various subject matter sectors.[81] Agency interests, however, were safeguarded by the same legislation which provided that the "share" of each agency would not be less than 85 percent of its previous year's total.[82]

In 1960, however, the Council approved in principle[83] the system of project budgeting recommended by the Technical Assistance Board,[84] and in 1961 it formally approved the proposal. At the same time it dropped the 85 percent provision.[85]

Thus there was a fairly high degree of built-in rigidity from the beginning. Even after the country programming procedure was adopted and project programming was adopted, the agencies were permitted to make overall proposals to Governments for the next financial period for up to 150 percent of agency programmes in the preceding period. They did not fail to do so. In effect, therefore, a firm foundation had been laid and maintained for the perpetuation of "agency shares."

It is interesting to note that, aside from relatively minor alterations to accommodate the participation of newly established specialized agencies, "country programming" produced very little difference in the relative distribution of resources among the participating agencies. Thus the relative "priorities" accorded to the principal sectors remained about the same over a period of nearly 20 years, no matter what system of allocation was in effect.[86] It can hardly be assumed that it was right for "priorities" represented in the programme to remain so relatively constant in such a rapidly changing economic, social and political environment.

On top of the constraints imposed by the multiplicity of programming authorities, there is the fact that participating agencies may offer packaged programmes to developing countries. These proposals justifiably derive from the basic terms of reference of the organizations concerned and are designed to implement their broad objectives. But they are not always tailored to the most immediate needs of the developing countries or to their capabilities and the prevailing conditions. Because they are not custom-tailored to actual interests and conditions, their use has led to frustrations and disappointments for all concerned. The direct transfer of techniques and concepts, without modification and without basic research on conditions and needs in the real world, is not likely to succeed in many instances, as has been amply demonstrated.

These constraints—some self-imposed—also apply generally to the field programmes of the agencies which are financed by their assessed budgets, the so-called "regular programmes." It has been seen that the total resources available under the regular programmes of the agencies somewhat exceed those of the technical assistance component of the UNDP. These programmes are not exactly parallel to those financed by UNDP, for they sometimes include activities and subject matter fields not now authorized under the UNDP terms of reference. They are, however, largely oriented to development problems and equally reflect the constitutional interests and priorities of the agency concerned. In this case also, developing countries may be encouraged to request a packaged product which may or may not be of real use or importance to them. The regular programmes, except that of the United Nations, are not subject to review and approval by the UNDP Governing Council, but are reviewed and approved by the governing bodies of the agencies.

The difficulties encountered by countries in planning and co-ordinating development activities, discussed in the previous section, also operate as constraints to flexible and informed programming. This general situation is complicated at times by the parochial special interests of individual ministries which, in the absence of effective central authority, act in concert with their opposite numbers in the multilateral agencies.

B—FINANCIAL CONSTRAINTS

Individual countries participating in the UNDP/TA component operate under a target constraint. Until recently, country targets were established by the UNDP Administrator and approved by the Governing Council for each financial period. Under the new "continuous" programming procedure, effective in 1969, targets are to be established each year to "apply to that year and provisionally to the three ensuing years."[87]

The country targets therefore determine the programme level for each country as far as the UNDP/TA component is concerned. The total amount available for the targets depends upon the voluntary

contributions pledged by Governments at the annual pledging confer-
ences. Adjustments in target figures are made from time to time. Thus
the 1969 targets showed "53 modest increases and 31 decreases of
which a few were significant, but many were no more than token
changes."[88]

The Special Fund component of the UNDP is not subject to the
same kind of institutional constraints that are involved in the technical
assistance component and to a considerable extent in the regular
programmes of the participating agencies. There are no country targets,
for example, and no "agency shares," although three large agencies
attained the same percentage share of Special Fund projects as their
shares in the 1968 TA programme; one large agency increased by 60
percent and another dropped considerably.

There is, however, an overall financial constraint arising from the
fact that there are many more requests for pre-investment assistance
than can be met by the present level of contributions. The selection of
projects for approval thus becomes a problem, especially in the light of
the general philosophy supporting United Nations programmes of
assistance which affirms that any country is, in principle, entitled to
participate in a multilateral programme. There is a general disposition
to spread the programme to as many countries as possible to achieve a
kind of geographic balance and "universality."

This problem has been discussed extensively at the fourth and
fifth Session[89] of the Governing Council and will be taken up again.

C—ELIGIBILITY AND CRITERIA

The question is discussed under the headings of "criteria for
determining eligibility" (of countries) and "criteria for the selection of
projects." The basic argument is whether most assistance should go to
countries which can use it best or to those which need it most. The first
group of countries are those which have established well-functioning
administrative structures, can provide counterpart personnel and technical services and have reasonable prospects for taking over the
maintenance and necessary follow-up of the project after UNDP
assistance is withdrawn. These countries may be reaching a stage of
development which is self-generating so that assistance can be used
effectively and economically. The group of countries at the other end of
the scale contains those which have not reached a self-generating stage
and do not possess the absorptive capacity required to make the best
use of international assistance. Yet their requirements are manifold,
and the argument is that their needs should have priority attention so
that they may more quickly be brought to an improved level of
development. There are, of course, many countries somewhere in
between the extremes mentioned.

There are also countries in which development has taken place to a point where there is a question of whether they continue to need multilateral external assistance or not, at least to the extent previously required. Yet they continue to request assistance, perhaps because they consider that it lends a certain amount of prestige to have an assortment of United Nations projects—one aspect of the universality doctrine. On the other hand, the programming agencies would likely be reluctant to cut back or eliminate programmes, especially by self-denying unilateral action. This would require explanations to their governing bodies and a partial repudiation of universality.[90] Wide geographic distribution of activities is generally considered an important and necessary objective.

There is no objective way to solve the problems of eligibility and selection. Such measures as per capita income, the level of which might determine the point at which assistance should be diminished or terminated, are not satisfactory for this purpose. There are many economic and social development objectives other than per capita income. Up to now, no satisfactory statistical method has been devised to compile a unitary "index of development" which might be used as an indicator of the need for external assistance.[91]

The method used so far in establishing criteria has been based upon the interpretation of the principles and criteria set out in General Assembly resolution 1240 (XIII). These refer to the desirability of large, not small, projects, to the necessity of giving due consideration to the urgency of the requests, to those projects promising early results with the widest possible impact leading in particular to new capital investment, to a wide geographic distribution, to problems of implementation, and to arrangements for the integration of projects into national development programmes and effective co-ordination with other multilateral and bilateral programmes.

Assuming that these criteria are applied with reason and flexibility, they do not provide specific guidance; their application does not guarantee that the "best" projects are chosen in particular cases or that the programme as a whole produces the "best" results. This conclusion is inevitable at present. An important constraint of an intangible and intractable nature still exists.

At its fifth session, the Governing Council, in reviewing the questions of eligibility of countries and the selection of projects, decided[92] among other things that the factors[93] used for the technical assistance component should be taken into account, that "countries which are relatively more developed should endeavour to increase their share of the cost of the assistance provided to them by UNDP including, when appropriate, the use of funds-in-trust arrangements" and "in the case of the most needy countries [that] counterpart contributions should be kept as low as possible and, in appropriate cases, the local cost requirements could be reduced or waived." The

Administrator is to report on the application of these guidelines at a later session.

These additional criteria may have the effect of spreading the available resources a little further and/or of relieving the "most needy" countries of some expenditure of national resources.

The development programmes of other members of the United Nations system, those programmes not under UNDP sponsorship, no doubt operate under very much the same constraint. There is not enough money to meet requests. Problems of the eligibility of countries and the selection of projects are similarly present.

D—ABSORPTIVE CAPACITY

The capability of many countries effectively to absorb international assistance is a long-standing and persistent problem. Basically, all United Nations programmes are joint ventures with national Governments and the multilateral agencies. These involve commitments by both sides to provide agreed resource inputs of various kinds at stated times and places. Unless these commitments are met, execution of the project becomes difficult or impossible.

Generally, countries are expected to provide counterpart officers, office space, secretarial and maintenance personnel, local transport, communication and other services, and, depending on the project, national currency for local employment and other local inputs. The ingredients of projects are very numerous indeed. While these requirements are usually agreed in advance in the work-plan or plan of operations, many difficulties are encountered in practice, some of which are not foreseen.

Short-falls in the capacity of countries to absorb assistance arise from several sources, many of them connected with the planning process itself and with administrative, financial and political problems in implementation.

Absorptive capacity does not refer exclusively to the joint ability of a country and an international agency successfully to complete a given project. In the case of training institutions and similar projects, for example, it is assumed that the institutes will be maintained more or less indefinitely by the national administration after the withdrawal of United Nations assistance. Experience has shown that many national Governments have not been able to assume financial responsibility at the conclusion of the original project.

Another aspect of national absorptive capacity refers to the sequential effects that may follow the successful completion of a project. A project is not usually an end in itself. For example, if the project results in the construction of a food processing plant, will the farm supply of foodstuffs be adequate, of the right quality, accessible in terms of distance and cost? Is there a market, a distribution system and credit facilities?

Both these examples, that of the training institution and the food processing plant, involve absorptive capacity in the broadest sense. Consideration of the probable sequential effects of a project, on the national budget or on other and indisputably related sectors of the economy, should be an essential part of the original planning exercise. Obviously, not all factors and relationships can be foreseen, but in many if not most cases, gross errors of judgement and decision can be minimized.

E—DELIVERY CAPACITY

The multilateral agencies also have difficulties in meeting their commitments. First among these is that of recruitment, which is becoming increasingly difficult. In many cases there is a delay of several months; in other cases the delay amounts almost to a year. There have been instances where the agency has had to admit that the post could not be filled. Various steps are being taken to overcome this problem, but it still persists.

The scheduling and delivery of equipment is a time-consuming process also, subject to delay in both procurement and transport. Many obstacles arise which could not have been foreseen by the agency concerned.

There is evidence that the substantive services of the operating agencies have not been able to keep pace with the growth of the programme, which between 1958 and 1968 increased six times.[94] This has meant that the critical processes of identification of needs, appraisal of requests, operational control and evaluation of results have not been systematically pursued. The magnitude of current operations has led in many cases to the sacrifice of forward planning activities and to an inability properly to foresee and follow up project results.

The administrative and substantive problems involved in the growth of the programme placed a considerable burden upon the capability of the agencies, which required them to re-group and reorganize their activities. Despite this, the Administrator of UNDP reported to the fifth session of the Governing Council that "It is clear that at the present time the capacity, at least of the principal agencies, is overtaxed by the responsibilities which they have accepted with respect to the present level of the programme."[95]

In light of this, and more particularly in light of a study of future needs for pre-investment activity, which for 1968-1970 showed estimated annual needs to be more than two and one-half times 1968 contributions,[96] the Governing Council authorized, on the recommendation of the Administrator, a "capacity study"—officially known as "A Study of the Capacity of the United Nations Development System." It is to be noted that the study covers both the operational programmes financed by the UNDP and other agencies of the United Nations system.

The study is to include an "inquiry into the character and content of the present programme and the modifications that may become desirable in the future . . . the most effective arrangements for the formulation, execution and the follow-up and evaluation of projects" and recommendations with regard to implications for the staffing and financing of the operational activities of the UNDP and the agencies.[97]

While it is not anticipated by many persons that the programme will grow by two and one-half times by 1970, the "capacity study" can make a very important contribution to the more effective formulation and management of the programme. As has been seen in earlier sections, programme planning with respect to both content and administration has not appeared to be unequivocally successful.

PART II: TO THE QUESTION OF METHODS AND TECHNIQUES

The analysis contained in part I of this study has shown in some detail the nature of the problems involved in efforts to evaluate the effectiveness of the development programmes of the United Nations system of agencies. There has been a persistent search over a number of years by administrators and scholars to find acceptable methods and criteria applicable to the wide variety of operational activities carried on by the international agencies.

As has been seen, the cause of the widely held concern about the effectiveness of the programmes and the degree of relationship to national needs lies mainly in unsystematic and unstructured programming and project selection. Most programming up to now has not been supported by an adequate information base which is essential for more rational approaches to planning.

In the following sections of this study, efforts are made to suggest methods and techniques which, if followed, would most surely minimize many of the uncertainties inherent in planning development activities. The suggested methods apply in the first instance to project preparation and to the appraisal of requests. Decisions must be made in each case as to what techniques would be applicable and how far it is justified to pursue them.

CHAPTER ONE

INTRODUCTION TO PERT NETWORK ANALYSIS FOR DEVELOPMENT PROJECT PLANNING AND CONTROL

Although fairly new to most national and international public operations as well as to most private industries, systematic planning and evaluation techniques, developed in the field of management science during the past decade, are in the process of replacing older methods which traditionally tend to obscure the overall picture and the complexities in the course of daily operations.

Increased technical and economic complexity in realizing successful development projects in general, and the necessity of co-ordinating and effectively utilizing inter-disciplinary and inter-organizational teams of specialists in particular, call for such planning techniques as will permit the accomplishment of given objectives under dynamic conditions and under the pressures of time and resources.

Moreover, effective management calls for control systems with fewer obstacles and in-transparencies and fewer dis-integrated planning and reporting procedures, in order to improve operations from a functional as well as an administrative point of view by improving inter-office and inter-organizational communications.

Several forms of network analysis are at present widely publicized as promising a series of evidently desirable accomplishments for projects of any size and complexity, including:

(1) rationalization of the planning process;

(2) improvement of communications, especially for complex inter-departmental and multi-organizational projects;

(3) increasing the probability of meeting deadlines;

(4) reducing planning, construction and operational costs;

(5) continuous and timely reporting of progress;

(6) timely identification of potential problem areas;

(7) providing for the managers possibility of focusing attention on the most critical sequence of activities in a particular project;

(8) proof of success;

(9) enforcing a discipline in planning, scheduling and reporting which is not accomplished as well with traditional methods.

The identification of specific conditions under which such promises could be realized (and, if at all, which ones most successfully and at what cost) is a question that remains to be analysed. If properly conceived, such an effort would constitute in itself a major operational-research project. Hence, the following presentation is not a report on pilot experimentation with network analysis (which, for example, would propose workable solutions to problems of planning constraints, quantification and other issues identified in part I of this study). The presentation is an introduction to the basic idea and to the essence of network analysis, including an illustrative example of a fairly typical UNDP feasibility study; it will in fact lead to the recommendation that such pilot exercises should be undertaken for the purpose of both (1) adapting and sharpening this tool in a United Nations environment as well as (2) helping the mutual understanding of the various independent efforts by United Nations agencies.

Several United Nations agencies are indeed engaged in designing network models for handling experts' reports, for example under the Technical Assistance component of the Development Programme (including aspects of data storage and retrieval). Agencies also are conducting pilot projects with the purpose of learning about network analysis, or projects on problems of internal administration, such as management surveys, payroll integration studies, etc. In connexion with the revised Special Fund reporting system, it was observed that its effective functioning "would depend largely on better project formulation, planning and supervision."[98] From this point of view, the use of modern programming and evaluation techniques (such as PERT network analysis) are also under consideration by several United Nations agencies.

Mention should be made of an earlier proposal which was submitted to the Committee for Development Planning at its second session by a member of this Committee.[99] The proposal contains an extensive presentation on how the basic management principle of network analysis may be adapted to assist countries in development planning, especially sub-regional planning and plan implementation. It concludes that the setting up of reliable time-oriented networks for project execution calls for skilled judgement on the part of the project managers and all other operational personnel involved; important channels of communication need to be established at the earliest stages of planning and programming; and in cases where a variety of interdependent projects and agencies are involved, such early communications can lead to even greater beneficial results. While reaching essentially similar conclusions, the section on PERT is for practical reasons concerned with the individual "project" as a unit of management and control.

A—THE BASIC IDEA OF NETWORK ANALYSIS

The approach assumes that a complex and dynamic situation under a manager's supervision can be understood as a whole network of material and non-material flows over time. Whenever such flows meet, there is a node which represents an intermediate functional step within the network. Networks are essentially *flow plans* which show diagrammatically the development of work over time. A project is first decomposed into tasks; the whole project is then presented as a series of interdependent events (or completed tasks) which are connected by activities (or: the necessary and sufficient material and non-material flows for the completion of events). It is a convention that the nodes (or events) are described as the start and completion of activities; arrows between events are symbols of time intervals.

For example, in figure 2, event 5 requires that activities 2-5 and 4-5 are both completed; event 5, in turn, requires the completion of activities 1-4 and 3-4, etc.

FIGURE 2

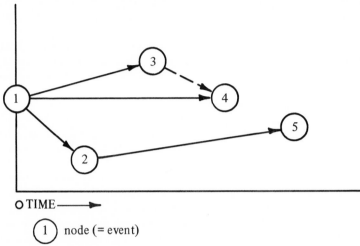

O TIME ⟶

(1) node (= event)

Definition An *event* is a point in time recognizable as a specific accomplishment

⟶ activity (time consuming)

— — — ➤ activity (non-time consuming)

Definition An *activity* is the work to be done within a given period of time in order to complete a given specified event. (Note that in special cases, the time period may be zero, and thus the activity non-time consuming).

In designing and planning a project, the planners' question is, then: which is the optimal network of activities and events leading to the desired and specified final event (or output of the project), and what kind of arrangements can be made in order to control such a network?

Some analysis has to precede an answer to this question. Not all lines in a network are equally important. There is above all a logical priority in arranging events which at first has nothing to do with time: for example, if an irrigation system is being constructed, it is evident that the electrical conduits can be installed at almost any time after the shells of the dam, the canal and the laterals have reached a certain degree of completion; whereas all locks have to be set and tested before water is directed into the reservoir and canal systems. Suppose that, in figure 2, events 4 and 2 are both logically necessary before event 5 can occur, but also that the completion of 4 takes longer than the completion of 2. It is then critical to the result that 4 be completed in the shortest possible time. More generally, if we look at time intervals $t_1, t_2, t_3, \ldots t_n$ of a given network, we observe that some of the sequences of intervals are more tightly packed with important activities and events than others. The actual network design will show that *one* pathway through the network is constituted of the most critical components in the sense of sequence of activities which together take the longest time: *the critical path*. A common experience which considerably complicates the problem at this point is the fact that the planning and controlling of this multiplicity of processes (expressed by "activities" and "events") involves only *some* degree, and by no means perfect certainty in knowing what the outcome will be. In other words, we are confronted with a complicated interplay of *stochastic processes*. The planner's and manager's problem is then to obtain, in advance as well as during the operation, sufficient information on the trend of the network and the phenomena that govern it.[100]

One particular model of network analysis has proved to be of special value for management decisions about projects which are (relatively speaking) one-time operations and which include a certain amount of identifiable sub-projects and component activities sequentially interrelated. In current literature this model is referred to as PERT/CPM. Both PERT (Program Evaluation and Review Technique) and CPM (Critical Path Method) were developed independently.[101] But, although each of the two techniques has still somewhat its own language, the difference between the two has all but disappeared. We shall not try to distinguish between the two methods, but shall refer to the entire approach as *PERT Network Analysis*.[102]

It is useful to separate two distinctly different stages of analysis fundamental to the approach: first, the planning stage, which includes the establishment of a functional work-breakdown of the project, the construction of the flow plan, the introduction of time estimates, explicit uncertainties and the identification of the critical path of the project; and second, the operational-control cycle, which includes the accumulation of time and performance data as the project is in operation, as well as periodic re-planning, adjustment and up-dating of the original network plan.

B—PLANNING: CONSTRUCTION OF THE FLOW PLAN

We recall that the design of a whole network of material and non-material flows (expressed by "activities" and "events") must pay attention to essentially two types of questions, (1) questions pertaining to logical priorities, and (2) questions pertaining to timing priorities. In other words, it is in the first place possible and necessary to assign priorities to all events within a given network on a purely logical basis, without information on the specific amount of time which activities require for completing these events.[103]

The subsequent illustration of some details of analysis at the planning stage is based on a Special Fund project entitled "Development of Rice Growing in the . . . River Basin."[104] The objective of this project is to assist the Government of the requesting country "in investigating and demonstrating the possibilities for irrigated rice production on a principal area . . . on the left bank of the . . . River."[105] First of all, the project should determine the form of rice-growing development which would suit the physical environment of the project area and the economic and social conditions of the country. A pilot irrigation scheme will be designed by the project staff and be constructed by the country's public works department. Moreover, special matters of irrigation layouts and techniques, crop water requirements, farm size, etc., will be tried under commercial conditions. Farm economic and organizational requirements for large-scale rice growing will be studied, with special reference to questions of farm size. The irrigation-development sub-project should also find specific information on economic and technological prospects for large-scale irrigation systems. Furthermore, the project will include an extension of the hydrological gauging programming of the . . . River and its tributaries. Hydrological data will be obtained for use in planning a pumping station, canals and other works (including an examination of flood control problems) required for the pilot irrigation project.

The project can first be broken down functionally into a series of sub-projects and sub-sub-projects which constitute the set of necessary and sufficient components of the whole. In the illustrative example, this means that the development plan of the . . . River Basin (which is the objective of the project) is composed of several functionally distinguishable sets of activities, including the collection of data and conducting of experiments with both an irrigation scheme, including flood control and hydrological services, and a rice-growing pilot farm. An economic and social appraisal of both of these pilot operations will then serve as the basis for formulating the development plan (figure 3). In a

FIGURE 3
Development of rice growing in the . . . River Basin:
functional work breakdown

. . . River Basin
Development Plan

Pilot Irrigation Scheme   Rice-growing Trial Farm   Economic and Social Appraisal

Flood Control Scheme   Hydrological Service

following step, the functional work breakdown should be developed further: the whole project should be analysed into separate tasks. In any real situation, the planner must decide how far such a decomposition into tasks must be developed. The list should then be revised into sequences of tasks, i.e., all activities and events of the project network should become presentable in their *logical sequence* by means of the flow plan. An example, in summary form, of this exercise for the project described above is given in figure 4. The flow plan now indicates that all activities must be performed in the order shown by the network. For example, activities succeeding any given event cannot be initiated before the immediately preceding activities have been completed. When finally time estimates are set into the flow plan, the critical path and schedule of the project can be identified.

The list of tasks, activities and events such as given in the flow plan for the whole project (figure 4) may be sufficient at, say, an over-all supervisory level. The nature of some tasks, however, may ask for further subdivisions. In such cases, of course, the listing of activities and events must be given in more technical detail. Take, for example, the portion of the whole project-flow plan concerned with hydrology and flood control, which is at the present stage provided for at a given level of detail (figure 5). With the same procedure applied in deriving the flow plan for the whole project, it is possible to carry the subdivision of tasks further to the appropriate level of detail. In the illustrative case, the partial flow plan given in figure 5 can be presented in the form shown in figure 6.

In general, given a master flow plan such as illustrated in figure 4, some of the main functional components (such as "hydrology and flood control," "rice-growing trial form," "economic and social appraisal," etc.), can be broken down into sub-networks with their own critical paths as necessary. This technique of hierarchies or "families" of networks provides a relatively simple means of dealing effectively with rather large numbers of tasks, since the preparation and management of sub-networks can be delegated to managers-in-charge and/or contractors.[106]

(i) *Critical path under certainty:*[107] The introduction of time considerations will now enable the identification of the most important component of the network: the *critical path.*

First of all, each activity is associated with a measure of duration. If, for example, the times required for the activities in the "flood control and hydrology" sub-network (figure 6) are known with certainty, the duration of this sub-project can be computed by means of table IX. In column 1 of the table, the activities are identified by the numbers of their predecessor and successor events; in column 2 the known activity durations are listed (in weeks); columns 3 and 4 list the number of weeks passed at beginning and completion of activities (note

FIGURE 4
Development of rice growing in the . . . River Basin:
decomposition of tasks and flow plan*

Events
1 Project declared operational
11 Project headquarters established
21 Construction equipment on site

Pilot Irrigation Scheme
13 Government data on pump station available
14 Flood control engineer in the field
15 Design information on pump station available
43 Pump station ready
44 Initial field visits, gauging station complete
51 Proposals for gauging stations and flood control measures complete
57 Final draft on flood control complete

58 Final draft on hydrology complete
59 Draft report on flood control and hydrology complete

Rice-growing Trial Farm
42 Farm and soils information complete
45 Farm information analysis complete
50 Irrigation-network farm ready for planting trials
60 Second field trials complete

Economic and Social Appraisal
49 Appraisal economist in field
66 Final field trials complete
70 Project wound up

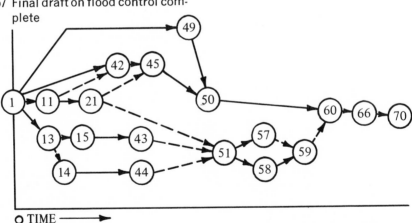

O TIME ⟶

* Time zero (event 1), in the above flow plan, is regarded as ''project declared operational'' (i.e., the actual start of field operations). Thus the network covers only the operational phase of the project. Pre-operational activities such as project identification, formulation and appraisal of requests, hiring of project manager, and other negotiations are not included. For reference, see Annex, process of project evaluation; flow plan by responsibilities.

FIGURE 5
Development of rice growing in the . . . River Basin:
partial flow plan

Events
51 Proposals for gauging stations and flood control measures complete
57 Final draft on flood control recommendations complete
58 Final draft on hydrology complete
59 Draft report on flood control and hydrology complete

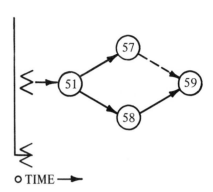

o TIME ➤

FIGURE 6
Development of rice growing in the . . . River Basin:
hydrology and flood control sub-network
hypothetical flow plan

Events
51 Proposals for gauging station and flood control measures complete
52 Gauging station improvement programme complete
53 Assessment of hydrological service complete
54 Initial flood control works complete
55 Final flood control studies complete

56 Up-grading of hydrological service complete
57 Final draft on flood control recommendations complete
58 Final draft on hydrology complete
59 Draft report on flood control and hydrology complete

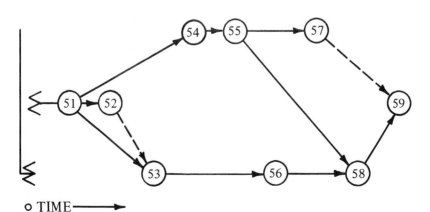

o TIME ➤

TABLE IX
Flood control and hydrology sub-network:
duration (in weeks) and critical path*

Activity (1)	Dura- tion (2)		Begin- ning (3)		Com- pletion (4)	Events on critical path (5)
51–52	20	+	53†	=	73	
51–53	5	+	53†	=	(58)	
51–54	25	+	53†	=	78	51,54
52–53	0	+	73	=	73	
54–55	40	+	78	=	118	55
53–56	70	+	73	=	143	
56–58	3	+	143	=	(146)	
55–58	40	+	118	=	158	58
55–57	2	+	118	=	120	
58–59	5	+	158	=	163	59
57–59	0	+	120	=	(120)	

* The values in this table are not related to an actual project and serve for illustration purposes only. Pro-forma of this table, cf. Richmond, *op. cit.*
† It is assumed that event 51 in the sub-network is completed 53 weeks after the beginning of the whole project, i.e., 53 weeks after time zero (= completion of event 1; see figure 4 above).

that it is assumed that the sub-project starts 53 weeks after the beginning of the main project). In cases where two (or more) activities are to be completed in the same event, beginning and completion of the next following activity are computed with the latest time-value obtained; the earlier times should be ignored (set in brackets). Thus, completion time of the longest path through the network is given by the highest value in column 4. Evidently, the sub-project cannot be completed before that time ("ceteris paribus"). The critical path of the network can then be identified by working backward from the final event, beginning on the bottom of the table, with activity 58-59, continuing with the preceding activity which is to be completed with event 58, eliminating the activities with completion times set in brackets, until the top of column 1 is reached. In the illustrative example, the critical path is found to be the sequence of activities through events 51-54-55-58-59 (column 5).

On the critical path, each activity begins *as soon as* its predecessor activity is completed (the linkage in the respective event being by definition *not* time-consuming). Yet, this is not necessary for any of the activities which are not on the critical path. For example, activity 55-57 takes two weeks and activity 57-59 takes no time; activity 55-58, however, takes 40 weeks and activity 58-59 five weeks. Thus, there is a "slack" time of 43 weeks on path 55-57-59 which indicates that the completion of these noncritical activities can be delayed up to 43 weeks without causing a delay in the completion of the whole network.

From this observation, two conclusions can be drawn, under conditions of certainty, with regard to resource allocation to the various tasks in the network. First, the execution of non-critical activities can be scheduled, *within* their leeway, for those periods of time which are the most economic ones compared to the resource requirements of the rest of the network. Secondly, if the project management seeks to shorten the completion time of the whole network without adding new resources, existing resources can be *shifted* from non-critical to critical activities. If new resources become available, they can be allocated to critical activities.[108]

(ii) *Uncertain time estimates:* The management of projects includes the manipulation of chance in the flow of time. Chance may permit the completing of an activity and thus the occurring of an event in less or more than the estimated time. Experience shows that time required to perform certain tasks will often vary, and that a large number of determinants may influence the length of this time. Anticipated environmental factors may be listed among such determinants as well as (and most importantly in the ex-ante stage) factors associated with procedures of estimating how much time each activity in the network will take.[109] From a probabilistic point of view, individual activity durations (t) and individual occurrence times (T) of events will be distributed around an average (mean) which denotes a value with the highest probability of occurrence. The risk of meeting a particularly pessimistic time decreases the longer the time is, while the chance of meeting a particularly optimistic time decreases the shorter the time is. In other words, the anticipated times of occurrence of given events may be understood as hypothetical and interacting probabilities, each centered on a mean with its associated distribution of frequency (variance) (figure 7). This means, furthermore, that two or more interacting situations are understood as dynamically interrelated in a way which can be measured and predicted by the use of probability theory.[110] Each event in the network, then, represents a measurable distribution of probabilities—a concept which now clarifies somewhat the initially introduced notion of the network as a complicated interplay of stochastic processes.

PERT network analysis is identified with a special procedure of handling the problem of chance with the help of probabilistic statements of activity duration. The analyst proceeds with the following steps:[111]

STEP 1: THE RAW DATA

On the basis of the flow plan (figure 6), time estimates should first be obtained from the responsible technical specialists.[112] In order to disassociate these specialists from a possible bias connected with

FIGURE 7

Chance and the occurring of events*

Time required to perform activities and thus the time of occurring of events will vary. Time of occurrence of an event can be understood as a hypothetical spectrum of probabilities.

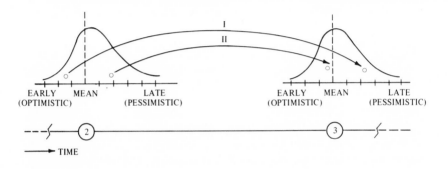

EARLY   MEAN   LATE   EARLY   MEAN   LATE
(OPTIMISTIC)   (PESSIMISTIC)   (OPTIMISTIC)   (PESSIMISTIC)

⟶ TIME

---

* See Beer, Decision and control, *op. cit.*, p. 174.

their knowledge of the actual schedule, and in order to gain more knowledge concerning the inherent variability of each activity within the network, three estimates for each activity should be obtained: a *most likely* elapsed time estimate (m) and two extreme values, an *optimistic* (a) and a *pessimistic* (b) one. A set of hypothetical estimates of this type is given in table X below.[113]

STEP 2: TRANSLATION OF RAW DATA INTO MEASURES DESCRIPTIVE OF UNCERTAINTY

The original PERT paper[114] presents a form of the calculus of variations for translating the raw data into statistical measures describing the expected elapsed time t^e (the mean) and the uncertainty involved in that expectation. This form is followed by most of the later papers on PERT network analysis.[115] The procedure is based on psychological studies done with technical specialists providing the raw data, and it assumes that the statistical distribution of such raw estimate approximates the beta-distribution. In other words, PERT assumes that the duration of an activity is a chance variable with beta-distribution. The extreme values, i.e., the optimistic and pessimistic estimates, are usually technically defined as times which under normal circumstances could be attained less than once in one hundred similar runs. Such considerations have led to the development of the following equations for translating the raw data into statistical measures of chance:[116]

FIGURE 8

Definition of t_e, T_o, T_E

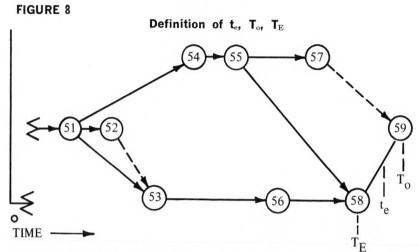

NOTE
t_e indicates the value of expected elapsed time (in weeks) associated with the interval between events 58 and 59. Similar values are associated with each activity (arrow) in the sub-network.
T_o indicates the expected completion time of the final event in the sub-network.
T_E indicates the expected completion time of event 58. Similar values are associated with each event (node) in the sub-network.

FIGURE 9
Hypothetical beta-distribution of performance time

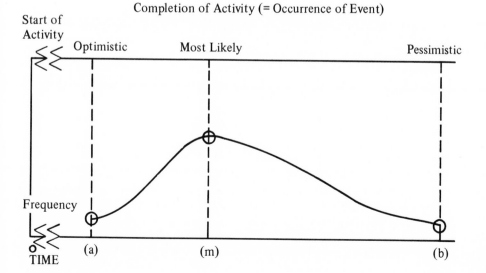

(1) expected time $t_e = \frac{1}{3} [2m + \frac{1}{2} (a + b)]$

(2) standard deviation $s = \frac{b - a}{6}$

(3) variance $s^2 = \left(\frac{b - a}{6}\right)^2$

Recalling briefly these first two steps, two possible sources of error in estimating time can be identified: (1) the quality of raw data, and (2) the appropriateness of the statistical apparatus for estimating expected times and uncertainty. Both of these components call for the development of experience, i.e., data on actual performance of raw time estimates as well as of the statistical formulization must be generated on the basis of pilot applications in order to refine the procedure at the planning stage before the approach becomes applied on a large scale in an area in which it was previously unknown.

The hypothetical values of t_e and s^2 computed with the PERT formulas 1 and 3 are included in table X.

STEP 3: PRESENTATION OF DATA IN ANALYTICALLY USABLE FORM

Having completed the investigating and calculating exercises of steps 1 and 2, it is possible to associate elapsed-time estimates and variances to each individual activity in the flow plan (figure 10). It is

TABLE X
Flood control and hydrology sub-network:
PERT time estimates (in weeks)*

Activity	Raw data			Statistical measures†	
	m	a	b	t_e	s^2
(1)	(2)	(3)	(4)	(5)	(6)
51–52	20	15	30	20.8	6.3
51–53	5	3	10	5.5	1.4
51–54	25	18	33	25.2	6.3
52–53	0	0	0	0.0	0.0
54–55	40	30	45	39.3	6.3
53–56	70	50	90	70.0	44.9
56–58	3	2	5	3.2	0.3
55–58	40	25	50	39.3	17.3
55–57	2	1	4	2.2	0.3
58–59	5	3	10	5.5	1.4
57–59	0	0	0	0.0	0.0

* The values in this table are not related to an actual project and serve for illustration purposes.
† The figures are rounded.

FIGURE 10

Network with elapsed-time estimates (t_e, s^2)

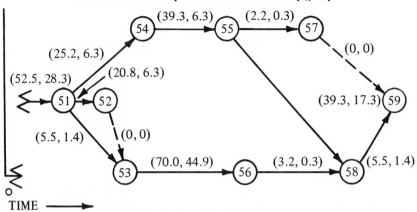

TIME ———▶

now necessary to present the information implicit in these data in a form suitable for analysis.

First, it is useful to order the events of the network sequentially on a row, starting from the final event until the present is reached (figure 11). The purpose of this rule is that no event be listed with one or the other of its successor events missing. The row is the point of departure for the analytical tables.

FIGURE 11   Sequential presentation of events

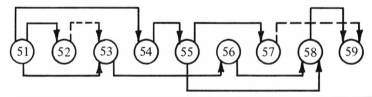

In the illustrative example, the assumption is made that the expected elapsed time until completion of all activities preceding event 51 is 52.5 weeks. This expectation is associated with a variance of 28.5 (see figure 10). Thus, the earliest expected time of occurrence of event 51 is 52.5 weeks after time zero, i.e., the time when the project (of which this sub-network is a part) actually gets started. It is now also possible to calculate cumulatively the earliest expected times (T_E) of occurrence and variances (s^2) for all events in this sub-network, from the origin to the final event (table XI). For example, the expected elapsed time (t_e) of activity 51–54 is 25.2 weeks and its associated variance (s^2) 6.3. Thus, the earliest expected time of occurrence (T_E) of event 54 is 77.7 weeks and the variance at this point 34.6. Attention must be paid to the number

TABLE XI

Cumulative tabular presentation of earliest expected time (T_E) and variance (s^2)

Events

	51	52	53	54	55	56	57	58	59
T_E	52.5	73.3	73.3	77.7	117.0	143.3	119.2	156.3	161.8($= T_0$)
s^2	28.3	34.6	34.6	34.6	40.9	79.5*	41.2	58.1*	59.6

* See footnote 117.

and time values of immediate *predecessor* activities and events; note, for example, that event 53 has two immediate *predecessor* activities, 51–53 and 52–53. Since activity 52–53 is non-time-consuming ($t_e = 0$) and, hence, event 52 can occur as late as (but not later than) event 53, it is the activity immediately preceding event *52* which must be taken into consideration for determining the earliest expected time of occurrence (T_E) of event 53. Since the question is to find the *earliest* expected time after time zero when event 53 *logically* can occur, T_E of event 53 must be calculated on the basis of the *largest* value among the predecessor activities, i.e.;

(1) $T_{E(53)} = T_{E(52)} = T_{E(51)} + t_{e(51-52)} = 52.5 + 20.8 = 73.3$ *weeks*
(2) $T_{E(53)} = T_{E(51)} + t_{e(51-53)} = 52.5 + 5.5 = (58.0$ weeks$)$
(3) The value under (1) is *larger* and therefore the earliest expected time of event 53.

Similarly, event 58 has two predecessor activities, 55–58 and 56–58:

(1) $T_{E(58)} = T_{E(55)} + t_{e(55-58)} = 117.0 + 39.3 = 156.3$ *weeks*
(2) $T_{E(58)} = T_{E(56)} + t_{e(56-58)} = 143.3 + 3.2 = (146.5$ weeks$)$
(3) The value under (1), i.e., 156.3 weeks, is *larger* and therefore the earliest expected time for event 58.

The variances for all elements are added along with the t_e values to determine the variance of the final event.[117]

It becomes again apparent from the above that some events can occur later than at their earliest expected times, without necessarily having an effect on the expected time of occurrence of the final event (T_o). On the basis of the collected data and flow plan, a set of values can be identified which indicates the *latest allowable times* (T_L) at which all events in the network must occur, if they should not cause slippage in meeting the final event. The individual values of T_L can be found by fixing the final event and working backward through the earlier events until the present (event 51) is reached (table XII).
For example:

$$T_{L(58)} = T_o - t_{e(58-59)} = 161.8 - 5.5 = 156.3 \text{ weeks}$$

and

$$T_{L(57)} = T_o - t_{e(57-59)} = 161.8 - 0.0 = 161.8 \text{ weeks}$$

Note that for this calculation the number of *successor* events and activities must be taken into consideration. For example, event 55 has two *successor* events and activities.

(1) $T_{L(55)} = T_{L(57)} - t_{e(55-57)} = 161.8 - 2.2 = (159.6$ weeks$)$
(2) $T_{L(55)} = T_{L(58)} - t_{e(55-58)} = 156.3 - 39.3 = 117.0$ *weeks*

It must be concluded that the *smallest* value, (2), is here the correct one, for if it were allowed to complete event 55 in 159.6 weeks after time zero, it would not be possible to complete the final event 59 after 161.8 weeks, but only after $159.6 + 39.3 + 5.5 = 204.4$ weeks.

TABLE XII

Latest allowable time (T_L) and "slack" (T_L-T_E)

Events

	51	52	53	54	55	56	57	58	59
T_L	52.5	83.1	83.1	77.7	117.0	153.1	161.8	156.3	161.8($=T_0$)
T_L-T_E ("slack" time)	0.0	10.5	25.1	0.0	0.0	25.1	42.6	0.0	0.0

Events with identical T_E and T_L values ($T_L - T_E = 0$) are *critical* for the performance of the network: the latest allowable times coincide with the earliest expected times at which such events can occur. Non-critical events, on the other hand, are those with different T_E and T_L values ($T_L - T_E > 0$). If the 162nd week is satisfactory for accomplishing event 59 ($T_o = 161.8$), the network can be fixed at that point and computed backward as described. It becomes evident that event 58 is critical ($T_L - T_E = 0$) and does not have any leeway or "slack" time such as event 56 ($T_L - T_E = 25.1$). The latter can again be scheduled at any position within its "slack" time range without jeopardizing the accomplishment of the final event 59. Thus, slack time (as defined above) can be understood as an indicator of scheduling flexibility which is given by a particular flow plan. The set of events and activities with no "slack" time is, of course, called the *critical path* of the network (figure 13).

FIGURE 13   **Identification of the critical path**

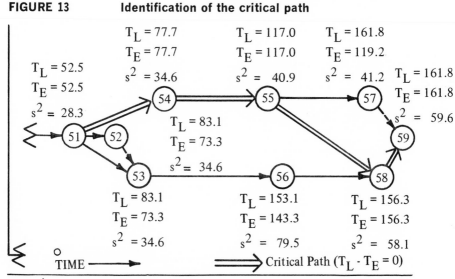

STEP 4: THE PROBABILITY OF MEETING A SCHEDULE

The PERT procedure assumes that the distribution for the *final* event in the network can approximately be expressed by a *normal* statistical distribution. Thus, given T_o and s^2, the probability of the final events occurring earlier or later than expected can be calculated.

Recalling that under conditions of a normal distribution about 68 percent of the sample will fall within the plus or minus one standard deviation and that, furthermore, approximately 16 percent fall below the mean minus one standard deviation, the probability that the final event will occur sooner than 154.6 weeks after time zero is 0.16.

Obviously, the probability of the final event occurring not later than 161.8 weeks after time zero is 0.5.

But suppose it is absolutely crucial that the final event will occur not later than within the 162nd week after time zero; clearly, the project manager cannot be satisfied with a probability of 0.5 for meeting this deadline. In such a case it is necessary to shorten the expected elapsed times of the network's most time-consuming activities. In fact, attention must be focused on the *critical path,* because it includes the network's most critical activities. The project manager will have to design an "optimum crash programme," i.e., a search for the most economical means of reducing the critical path and thus reducing T_o in the network. The more T_o can be reduced, the higher the probability of meeting the deadline in the 162nd week. But usually a reduction of the critical path is accompanied with an increase in cost. Thus, the value of increasing the probability to 0.6, 0.7, 0.8 at increasing marginal costs must be evaluated and decided upon.

It is not suggested that analysis always precedes the setting of deadlines. In fact, in many of the cases the very opposite may happen. The project manager can be faced with "exogenous" deadlines which may or may not be possible to meet. The analyst will then have to compare the given deadlines with the "endogenous" constraints of the project which become evident through PERT network analysis, and make probabilistic statements on the possibility of meeting the former. For example, suppose a deadline is set at the end of the 147th week after time zero for completing event 59 (T_os:148.0). Analysis has shown that completion may be expected during the 162nd week (T_oE:161.8). What is the probability of meeting this deadline? (See figure 14). A numerical answer to this question can be obtained, if *first* the absolute value of the difference between expected-completion time and deadline time is divided by the standard deviation for the expected-completion time, and *second* the result is converted into a probabilistic statement:

(1)
$$\frac{1}{{}^s T_{oE}} \left| (T_{oS} - T_{oE}) \right|$$

$$\frac{1}{\sqrt{51.3}} = 13.8 = \textit{1.91}$$

(2) Using the Normal Curve Table for Probability-P, the value 1.91 corresponds to a probability P = 0.028 approximately. In other words, there is a chance of less than 3 percent of meeting the pre-set deadline in this example. It is thus reasonable to assume that the schedule is in question. Relatively high values (0.5 or more), in turn, indicate that the deadline can be met.

FIGURE 14

The probability of meeting a given deadline*

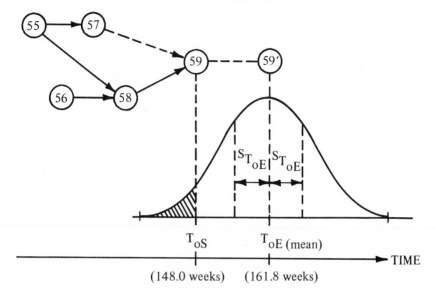

T_{oS} given deadline for completion of event 59
T_{oE} expected time of completion of event 59 (59')
$^sT_{oE}$ standard deviation of expected-time value
shaded area is a graphical measure of probability of completing event 59 on or before T_{oS}

* Cf. Malcolm et al., *op. cit.*, p. 658; slightly modified.

C—OPERATIONAL CONTROL: MONITORING AND RESCHEDULING

Some of the considerations on probability at the planning stage give rise to the initial hypothesis that a project under PERT network analysis is entering very different situations during its operational stages. Whereas the former is mainly dealing with given sets of variables, constraints and assumptions, it is the latter which is now concerned with absorbing dynamic processes involving change, challenges of schedules, formulation of new networks, with continuous revision of plans and even of objectives as time and operation go on.

The general philosophy of the notion "operational control" implies a device which in literature is often referred to as a *management control system*. This is most usefully based upon a model which understands management (1) as a design and decision problem under varying degrees of uncertainty, using both past experience and available data, and (2) as a process of learning from results of decisions and adding the results to a memory unit for the perusal of future decision problems. A management control system is, then, the institutionalized and routinized assimilation of past results into the body of knowledge which is used for subsequent decisions.[118]

PERT network analysis requires such a management control system. Condition for the applicability of PERT is that analysis of the original plan can still proceed in the light of on-going operations. Moreover, the system should be able to indicate the relative value of potential courses of action whenever decisions have to be made under changing operational conditions. The system's effectiveness is indicated by the speed with which unforeseen situations can be recognized and operations adjusted accordingly. For example, the network analysis applied to the 1967 World Exposition in Montreal was specifically designed for continuous monitoring, changing and adjusting of all phases of work on the world's fair, i.e., from original feasibility studies of individual sub-projects, through all phases of architectural and engineering design, to the actual construction and, after the Exposition had closed, the eventual demolition. A total of more than $750 million worth of work was scheduled for design and construction within a period of three and a half years and was closely monitored with a computerized network model. The initial network data were stored in an IBM 1401 computer. Every week, progress report information was submitted by individual contractors and prepared for computer input. The computer then compared the weekly progress information against the stored network data. For the eventual changes in the network itself, an IBM 1620 computer was used for the necessary calculations. It is reported that the time- and resource-saving importance of the network approach became evident from the beginning. In one case, for example, the network showed that a contractor building a vital access bridge would complete construction behind schedule. Thanks to early identification of this problem, an extra $7,000 in resources was allocated to this sub-project. The bridge was completed on time, and alternative plans for the construction of $200,000 worth of temporary ramp facilities elsewhere could be cancelled.

The basic tools for analysis during on-going operations are already developed at the planning stage. In addition, analysis can display the options available to the project manager of (1) implementing adjustment and trade-off plans and of choosing schedules, resources and technical specifications, or of (2) testing implications of different decisions by computer simulation. For example, the search for the most economical means of reducing the critical path may illustrate this point. In fact, for all but very elementary networks, operational control "by hand" may turn out to be too costly; only with a suitable computer model does it become possible to study the behaviour of highly complex networks and derive useful conclusions within a reasonable amount of time. For example, in the application of PERT network analysis to the construction of the European nuclear reactor ESSOR, a special computer programme was developed for dealing with this "crash" problem. It was necessary to reduce T_0 of a series of technical experiments within the project (which were expressed by a separate sub-network) from 11 to nine weeks; in other words, the critical path was to be reduced by two weeks. The first question in such case is whether a reduction is at all possible. If it is impossible, one can only accept an inevitable delay and its consequences. If a reduction is possible, it is usually not sufficient to confine the adjustment to the critical path, because the allowances ("slack" times) of other activities which are not on the critical path may not be large enough to absorb the reduction of T_0, and the critical path of the network may change altogether. A research article on this project concludes that once a computer programme for coping with such a problem has been developed and used, the advantage of the computerized PERT procedure is that each "run" provides the necessary elements of decision. Any decision in turn modifies certain elements within the network which automatically call for new calculations. If the model shows that a reduction in T_0 can be implemented in several alternative ways, it is possible to make choices on the basis of the estimated costs of alterations.[119]

The process of systematic alteration of the original plan as the project is in operation is often referred to as "up-dating," i.e., the securing of current information on time estimates for activities in progress, possible revisions of estimates for activities yet to be performed (which now can presumably be provided more accurately) and the consideration of time, resource and technical information on possible new activities and events to be included in the network. On the basis of such information, anticipated changes and problem areas can be indicated so that corrective action can be taken.[120] Rescheduling of the project, then, usually implies an extension of the date scheduled for the final event.

The basic rules for performing this adjustment are shown in figure 15. If the rescheduled completion date of the final event is changed, the latest allowable times for all events must be recalculated. If the latest allowable time of a given event preceding the final event turns out to be shorter than the earliest expected time, the rescheduled date must be set at the latest allowable time; otherwise it must be set within the "slack time" interval.[121] Scheduling and rescheduling should be decided upon according to an established policy regarding the probability to be assumed in meeting scheduled and rescheduled dates.

Note, however, that a simple extension of the date scheduled for the final event may not be sufficient to absorb the delay which has developed from the beginning. First of all, even if the manager has insisted on operating within a range of high probabilities, the worst can still happen. It is unlikely, but not impossible, that one or the other of the events within the network will exceed the earliest expected time by a margin much wider than anticipated. Secondly, a relatively small delay may well become amplified into an excessive delay.[122] The original critical path then becomes obsolete, and a new one must be calculated and all parts of the system adjusted accordingly.

D—Some Remarks in Perspective

Most analyses of economic decision problems can be classified into two currents of thought which are sometimes confluent, sometimes in conflict: (1) the "programming" approach, which implies choice in advance and in principle once and for all of the value of a certain number of decision variables; and (2) the "strategy" approach, which implies that projects, planned and decided upon in advance, should be completed by new projects which are inspired by new circum-

FIGURE 15

Rules for rescheduling

A. Situation

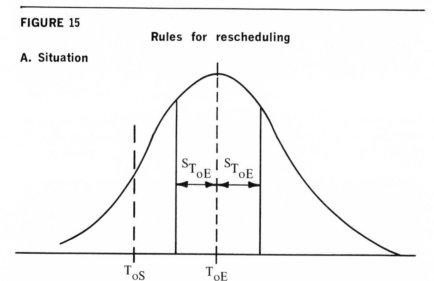

T_{oS} Originally scheduled completion time of final event
T_{oE} Expected completion time of final event based on new analysis

B. Rules 1. set $T_{oS} = T_{oE}$
2. recompute T_L values of all events preceding the final event
3. schedule all predecessor events
    3.1 where $T_L < T_E$, set $T_L = T_E$
    3.2 where $T_L \geq T_E$, set $T_E \leq T_S \leq T_L$

stances.[123] Although in development planning the theoretical question regarding the possibility of considering new information *during* the process of plan implementation is open,[124] PERT and related forms of network analysis have moved toward actually combining both approaches. Although "programmed" and thus a theory of choosing in advance, PERT implies a systematic approach to multi-period decision-making, including the handling of decision-learning situations. In other words, what one decides at any particular stage, from experience and available data, becomes modified as each stage in the process passes and additional information and experience is used.[125]

Beside the theoretical considerations, this raises a number of practical problems. The object of project planning and control of the network type, and thus of the PERT approach, is the prediction of problems. Hence, the subdivision of projects into relatively short and controllable elements is important in order to facilitate timely corrective action. Managerial rule of thumb is that it is better to be 100 percent wrong after a two-week period than 20 percent wrong after one year. However, "timely corrective action" is only possible if a fast, reliable communication and control system is concurrent with operations. The fact that a multiplicity of offices and organizations (financing agency, operating agency, recipient Government) are engaged in the planning and operation of projects does not facilitate the design and functioning of such a system.

A number of project-reporting pro-formas are proposed throughout the PERT literature for weekly, monthly and quarterly flows of information and up-dating.[126] The particular form and timing of communications, of course, is to a large extent determined by the project itself and by its institutional environment. No form, however, will replace the willingness of the particular groups concerned to actually co-ordinate their efforts effectively. Moreover, the objectives of the project must be made clear in order to make a sound functional work breakdown possible in the first place. Yet the more heterogeneous the constituents of a project operation, the more diffuse and numerous may be its objectives. Thus, perfect clarity of objectives and the possibility of complete rationality of all activities and events within a network is probably an exception rather than the rule.[127]

The relatively simple logic of the PERT approach may prove to be still insufficiently developed for coping with very complicated logical structures which may underlie the various uncertainties of given development projects. Experiments with network analysis have to be, and in fact are, widely connected with the search for the appropriate modifications in the particular new field of application.[128] One recent paper, for example, was specifically concerned with expanding the capability of PERT network analysis for handling more complex structures of uncertainty.[129] Nevertheless, the introduction of any applied technique of operational control should not overemphasize the adaptation of existing techniques or the creation of new models at the expense of a carefully designed implementation plan. For the purpose of the latter, the following phases are most usefully distinguished:[130]

(1) Preparatory Phase
    Briefing for Management
    Pilot Application, Phase I
    Pilot Application, Phase II
    Monitoring and Critique

(2) Organization for Large-Scale Implementation

With respect to the preparatory phase, it must be noted that oversimplification of pre-conditions, insufficient knowledge and training, poor briefing of top-level management and, in general, inadequate development of the system can indeed result in failure to exploit its potentials, if not in total disappointment.

First of all, the choice of suitable pilot projects is of prime importance. They should be large and complex enough to display some of the system's potentials and advantages, but not so large as to introduce serious difficulties to a still relatively inexperienced group of pilot personnel.[131] A first phase of the pilot exercise should consist of testing the feasibility of the concept as a potential system. This includes the preparation of the work breakdown and first sufficiently detailed flow plans.[132] The first actual collection of time estimates from the competent specialists (raw data) will reveal the communication problem, as well as the need to set re-planning, adjustment and up-dating procedures in motion. The actual monitoring process of a pilot project is then at the same time a test of the pilot communication and management control system designed for the purpose of the pilot exercise. Furthermore, a system of collecting performance data on all aspects of the exercise must be included (i.e., training, performance of estimates, capability of actually keeping timely control, identification of potential problem areas, etc.), but above all the performance of ex-ante and on-going analysis as described in this chapter. A thorough assessment of this first phase of the pilot exercise should include, moreover, an evaluation of the costs and advantages of the system that is designed.

A second phase of the pilot operation may then include (1) the actual design of an operating system for collection of the data, selection of reporting periods, final design of forms and other means of communication and (2) the development of a computer programme for simulation and control purposes such as illustrated above.[133]

The actual organization of large-scale implementation, then, depends on several variables, including (1) the particular purpose of applying the planning and control technique in a given environment, (2) the findings and experience drawn from pilot exercises, (3) the specific training requirements and (4) the design of the actual data-processing and communication system. Observations on that complex of problems are beyond the scope of this study.

CHAPTER TWO

COST-BENEFIT ANALYSIS FOR PROJECT EVALUATION

A—MODELS FOR ANALYSIS

Cost-benefit analysis will be discussed in a way that emphasizes its practical applicability in project formulation and implementation, without straying too far from the logical and theoretical rationale of the technique.

The exercise of analysing projects to determine or assign discounted values to their expected streams of costs and benefits, and in comparing these to provide information to aid a decision on the desirability of given projects, presupposes the defined project or programme itself. "Project" in turn is equivalent to the generalized sense of "production" and the organized activity during which resource inputs are converted into other resource outputs in determinable time periods.

Usually there is an assigned "project length of time" covered by the budget. The usual expression for the conversion of inputs to outputs during this project period is a short- or long-run "production function." A production function is a mathematical statement of the technical relations governing a production process. In its most general form it equates quantities of output with those of the factor inputs such as labour, land and capital necessary to produce them. Nevertheless, even after specifying the variable input factors and parameters or constants for particular functions in their practical application, production functions are abstractions from actual production processes of the projects to which they are applied. They call in practice for estimations of the values used for analysis, to be made from regression analysis methods applied to several observations. For the short-run function the inputs are assumed fixed and the economic time horizon goes as far as the primary and direct expected set of outputs which should be identified in the project work-plan in the context of the stated objectives and targets. For the long-run function, however, the inputs are not assumed fixed. Nor is the subsequent life of the outputs (i.e., their expected effects over a period of years in given sectors of the economy or in their operation and maintenance) as part of the on-going long-run "project" being analysed. In consideration here are projects that are refinanced or extended or somehow continued beyond the project time length of the initial plan. New inputs become applicable together with any unobligated portion of the original budget as well as leftover equipment. On the outputs side too, secondary and indirect effects of the outputs of the completed phases of the project are analysed in order to evaluate total benefits or effectiveness.

The problem of identifying inputs and outputs and their sequential flows is one important reason for insisting on a PERT type of network approach to project implementation control, with the effective and certainly practical treatment of "uncertainty" which the technique allows. There are as discussed above the three time estimates leading to the use of the beta-distribution approximation to compute the most likely due-date for the projected output, as well as the provision for the periodic re-examination and redrawing (as necessary) of the project control network and for the correction of any discrepancies in timing of input-output streams during actual implementation. This immediate feedback to the on-going project would clearly seem to be the most practical way to use data deriving from project implementation and from the expert, mission or other reports which often accompany the implementation process.

One illustration of how complicated the considerations necessary for adequate identification can become may be seen in the case of continued training programmes of the technical assistance type. If one of these is viewed from the earlier period or periods as "a project" for purposes of analysis, some of its main "output"—the trainees—may become "input" in assistance or supervisory roles, each with salary and allowances and training equipment as well as the plant of the training establishment to which they are attached. Others of the trainees find jobs in which their contributions can be more directly accounted for in systems designed to analyse more than the original project. One project had envisaged as an initial phase the training of some 600 persons in a five-year period. In fact, about 700 persons had been trained in the first two years of the programme to satisfy the demands of the accelerated agrarian reform programme. Obviously, any pre-implementation mathematical models of the project would have had to be done many times over if they were to be useful representations of the actual operation. This means that for the above example, the models would have to be adjusted or recast at various points in time, to take account of whatever new inputs became available to make possible the 100-man jump in trainee output, even though the project had three years to run as per the initial plan. These readjustments are necessary to approximate, as accurately as practicable, a systems-analytic view of the project in the sense of an integrated set of input vectors ("X") yielding output vectors ("Y") during time periods "T," given the operating structure and organization of the project.

For any project for which "n" inputs and for example "m" outputs could be identified from PERT network models of its implementation, ideally a general form of the elements of the production function would be $X = (x_1, \ldots, x_n)$ $Y = (y_1, \ldots, y_m)$, where the subscripts represent the "i^{th}" input or "j^{th}" output for equivalent stated time periods. For given numerical values possible from legislative, economic and engineering considerations, arrays of (X, Y) would emerge, where (X, Y) in more detail could be made up of elements of the form (x_1, y_1), (x_1, y_2), (x_1, y_3), $\ldots$ where y_2 or $y_3 \geqslant y_1$ in common (monetary) values. It is in this context that one could define efficiency[134], since with the inequality above and assuming that $y_1, y_2, y_3, \ldots$, were equally desirable outputs, if only for different society groups or sectors, the (x_1, y_1) pair would clearly be relatively wasteful or inefficient. Such considerations would apply in the piecemeal analysis of the activity paths of each network; the latter as models of alternative implementation approaches being of course the objects to be compared in terms of the expected and relative benefit-cost ratios and net-benefit values which would be the end results of the cost-benefit analysis exercise at the pre-implementation phase.

Another way would be to say that, given the planned or budgeted inputs of the project and their scheduled period of input for discounting purposes as well as the expected outputs according to the objectives identified as targets, scalar-valued functions of the general form $U(X,Y)$ could be constructed to order all the possible and probable plans for carrying out the project. This would include an array from the most to the least desirable implementation plan, each of which would fulfill the project objectives by alternative implementation approaches. Parallel orderings in terms of increasing net-benefit value and benefit-cost ratio estimates would also be called for at this stage, as aids in the choice of the particular project plan to be implemented. Questions about the possibility or validity of such a quantitative "U" function are not really insurmountable, if one considers its restricted "degrees of freedom" once (X,Y) are identified. The realization that this determinateness is quite general once criteria are set can be surprising. Their form, always is a function of a cost: benefit ratio, as Thomas (1963)[135] has shown, is even more so. Thomas concluded flatly, although he drew from the area of environmental control, that "the fixing or setting of quality criteria [for control of the environment] always involves a value judgement, and this value judgement always has the form of a cost: benefit ratio: *"To set a criterion is to impute a cost: benefit ratio."*

The actual value of the ratio can always be questioned, of course. The point nevertheless is that if, for example, $1.2 million were earmarked together with a $.9 million counterpart contribution for five years to do research and train personnel in the management of co-operatives in a particular country project, the equivalent could be usefully shown as a mathematical relationship with a parameter "U," which could then logically be called the value in human or any other terms of co-operatives to that country in terms of the given project.

The project criteria and ultimate stated outputs at each node of the PERT network would of course be determinable from the objectives and targets which come with its authorization. In effect we always have so much budgeted inputs for the purpose of attaining such-and-such targets spelling out the overall project objectives. The manner and extent to which the targets are to be attained set intended standards or criteria; and the point is that it is usually possible analytically to point to so much resources used to attain such targets and to such tolerances or criteria. The meaningfulness in any given instance of the needed (money) valuations of project yield is clearly not susceptible to any general proof or justification. Discussion here concerns strictly the issue of the analytic possibility or otherwise of their very imputation.

To repeat, then, for any project for which a finite outlay is budgeted for a given period and purposes, a cost–benefit analysis in terms of their mutual determination (input to output) is implicitly possible. A further example is in order to point up the logical necessity of the approach, which nevertheless could be viewed in other senses as an absurdity. In comparison with a $4.2 million training programme adapted to the problems of rural life including provisions of health care, another project with counterpart contribution of over $7.0 million for a $9.0 million institute of health would yield a possibly different valuation of individual health. Possible values of their respective outputs could already differ from the difference of their respective mandated objectives and targets. Different countries apply different levels of similar input for varying national schemes; this simply means, for analytical purposes at least, different valuations of benefits, human or otherwise. If a region in Brazil budgets for a lower level of inputs into a water project than does another in New Zealand and both aim at approaching the same WHO standard of a maximum allowable cyanide concentration of 0.01 milligram per litre, it is reasonable to ask whether people in Brazil should drink less pure water than those in New Zealand. "If the answer is not yes (and Brazil must spend much more for the purest water) then it must be asked whether they would not thereby be deprived of resources that might better go into highways, schools or into other sectors. . . ."[136] In practice, the value of such international comparisons is very limited, because their validity is caught up in the unsolved index number problem which in turn has often led to a resort to sensitivity analysis and shadow pricing, with generally still unsatisfactory results.

Getting back to the general net-benefit function, $U(X, Y)$ could be expressed as equivalent to $\sum p_j y_j - \sum \bar{p}_i x_i$ where the bar superscript represents the average value of the corresponding (by subscript) output and input. In practice, p_i and p_j, especially the latter, would in turn be functions of (X, Y), properly taking into account the relevant probability distribution of the output values. A better form of the objective function would then be EU(X, Y) to emphasize as criterion the expected value of net benefits. For actual "E" values, the PERT computation of variance "s^2" values discussed above as measures of the uncertainty associated with each project activity are directly applicable in the determination of the value of "E" for the net-benefit function. Reserving our discussion of discounting, let us assume as constants a going discount rate, r, representing the opportunity cost of capital, the unit price, p, and the length of life of the project, T. Then, from the usual form of the formula for the present value of expected future streams of value, the present value of scheduled varying inputs would be $[1 - (1 + r)^{-T}] \sum \bar{p}_i \bar{x}_i$, and of outputs, $[1 - (1 + r)^{-T}] \sum \bar{p}_j \bar{y}_j$. The planned production would then show a net benefit of

$$[1 - (1 + r)^{-T}] (\sum \bar{p}_j \bar{y}_j - \sum \bar{p}_i \bar{x}_i)$$

At this point we reiterate that, whenever a project is proposed with explicit objectives to be achieved with given resources and these objectives are classified for incorporation into mathematical models of appropriate generality relating the objectives or "quality criterion" to the estimated and discounted costs (taking into account the effects of all relevant engineering and economic factors), then the assignment of numerical values to the quality criterion which follows ultimately from the project proposal itself should always allow an implicit utility parameter (human or otherwise) or benefit vector to be computed. At worst, which is probably the rule rather than the exception, the money valuation of some of the benefits or outputs is "impossible" or at least demonstrably unreliable. Such outputs could then be treated as residuals on the plus side, i.e., as complements of the identified and already priced outputs, and then all against the inputs costs. The results of the cost–benefit analysis would then take the form, for example, of recommendations to the decision-maker to the effect that whatever the residual benefits, they would have to be valued at a present value of "x" money units in order for an estimated positive net benefit value or a benefit–cost ratio of at least unity to be achieved.

An example of "quality criteria," in the most general sense of the insistence on the operational meaning of project objectives, could be the establishment of a water management office in a country to help establish an organization to co-ordinate and control the development of all water resources throughout the country. For analysis, this could translate into the collecting, classifying and relating of data such as the following:

(1) "X" legal and other experts working "Y" hours a day for "Z" months at $"L" a month to prepare a national water policy document;

(2) "M" experts working . . . to reorganize and work to set up a water resource inventory centre. (In turn, such a centre has more detailed criteria, e.g., the specific items it must include . . . by very definition.)

Somewhere the detailing has to stop, either because of time and budget constraints or because of lack of information, but even this point could be very remote. And it is at this point that use of the modern digital computer is often the only way to model and simulate the interaction of the numerous factors which go into the given project, especially if the project is a very complicated one.

The foregoing statement calls for a number of more detailed practical considerations relevant to the application of cost-benefit analysis. First, recapitulating the procedural steps, there is the listing and classifying of the inputs and expected outputs of alternative project implementation methods, and their use in the design of integrated models or plans of whole implementation processes. Then there is the construction of production functions relating the discounted values of the inputs to the expected outputs. These functions would be in forms to yield on manipulation or rearrangement, particular benefit:cost ratios for whatever utility parameters the decision-makers are interested in. The additional ranking of all possible project–plan models by net benefit function, and therefore the extent to which project objectives would be fulfilled, would give decision-makers an option to skirt the debate about whether or not to maximize the difference between the sum of benefits and costs rather than the ratio of the two. The implication, in our opinion, would be a lack of a generally valid decision rule for or against either the absolute aggregate difference or the ratio. Caution is necessary even with the pre-implementation of project cost-benefit analysis consideration of alternatives.[137] It is true that the sequential consideration of the widest range of alternative ways of reaching stated objectives would logically give the greatest scope for the application of the efficiency criterion in choosing the way to make the actual expenditure. But project design, mathematical model-building even with the aid of digital computers, and the calculation of net-benefit are all time-consuming and expensive activities in themselves. Usually there is also lack of information, so that it is safe to say that not only are all possible alternatives never analysed, but they could never be.

B—What Costs and What Benefits?

The listing and classification of the inputs and expected outputs tackles of course the usual question of what costs and what benefits are to be included?[138] On the input side, the actual inputs to be "costed," "priced" or "assigned monetary values" vary from project to project. In this connexion one should take a close look at the budget constraint. Its strength as a constraint varied by type of input. Expert salaries can be clearly fixed, relative, for instance, to the costs of keeping major items of equipment in operation for the implementation of the project, in climates, for example, where there is no history of their performance characteristics. This is why the actual project implementation model, in PERT network form and corrected as necessary, should be the basis of the complete costing of the inputs and outputs. The prior estimation of the extent of use of particular inputs would then be compared with the budget allocation for them, and if necessary would scale down objectives accordingly. Otherwise it should be no surprise that many projects turn out under-budgeted, or have to continue much beyond their projected deadlines.

C—UNCERTAINTY

Problems with "uncertainty" arise in two main ways on the input side. In the first place, there are many reasons why an input that was planned for might not in fact be available for use at its scheduled time. Secondly, the input could under-fulfil its planned contribution to the production process. These problems can be at least partially compensated for by the mathematical expectation, E, factor in the input vector. For most durable equipment the manufacturers could be expected to suggest reasonable numerical values from their own reliability tests. For other inputs a range of values may be obtained from observations in similar or comparable situations.

On the output side, problems of recession in time and space and therefore lack of information are compounded with those of failure. The information lack problem (of which the use of erroneous information is an aspect) is a general one which the analytical process itself is in a sense constantly trying to resolve, never succeeding. As a result, nobody ever lists all possible costs and benefits because they are not all known, for one thing. Often only the most immediate direct costs and benefits are counted because the secondary ones are not known, nor are possible links between the two or between them and other possible benefits. The time dimension is an additional confounding factor, and the stopping point of any tracing of the direct and indirect effects of any project through time have to be decided more or less arbitrarily. As has been well stated,[139] "Induced productivity effects in particular (like those resulting from better housing or health), may take generations to work themselves out. But here as with certain other problems of coverage, difficulties of setting time-boundaries converge with those of evaluation . . . and incline the analyst to choose in practice a time period governed by the physical life of the project (sometimes as determined by legislation) and the availability of information."

The practical importance of the issue of direct and indirect benefits as well therefore as "externalities" and "spillovers" has been underlined in the Prest and Turvey survey.[140] When is it necessary to include the effects on the output of "B" goods of a project to produce "A" goods? Clearly, when "A" happens to be an upstream dam and "B," "C," . . ., other dams actual or projected relatively downstream and for whose operations the water levels maintained at "A" would be crucial. Thus legitimate external effects to be taken into account are those "that alter the physical production possibilities of other producers or the satisfactions that consumers can get from given resources," but *not* side effects whose sole impact is through the prices of products or factors. The idea is to avoid double counting and eliminate purely transfer or distributional items from the analysis, emphasizing "the value of the increment of output arising from the given investment" rather than any increment in the values of existing assets identifiably affected by the project. Thus, one could count the benefits of increased energy production in the downstream dam following the construction of a reservoir upstream, but not for example the greater profitability of garages or restaurants (or a newly improved road), employment of more labour by them, higher rent, etc. The reasoning is that these benefits could not be credited to the road investment as such, "even if the extra profitability of the garages on [this] road is not offset by lower profitability of garages on another, which are now less used as a result of the traffic diversion. Any net difference in profitability and any net rise in rents and land values is simply a reflection of the benefits of more journeys being undertaken than before, and it would be double counting if these were included too." The principle may be a most useful one, although there could also be endless controversy in the application to actual cases, where once again legislative or time constraints or lack of information may have to rule as to the cutoff point of the count of benefits.

D—PRICING

The valuation at the time of the cost-benefit analysis of a project of the stream of costs and benefits which the work plans of the project call for is the problem. Since the various time streams cannot be expected to be shaped similarly, they have to be made comparable for convenience of computation by transforming each to its present value. Thus the real problem shifts to one of finding the appropriate rate, "r," at which to discount future inputs and outputs with the usual formula: $\dfrac{1 - (1 + r)^{-T}}{r}$, as we saw above. Steiner[141] calls this "r" "the opportunity cost of deferred consumption," sometimes called "social time preference." He distinguishes it from other interest rates that better recommend themselves in other areas such as the following:

(1) the Government borrowing rate;

(2) the private borrowing rate;

(3) the opportunity cost of transferring funds from the private sector to the public sector;

(4) the internal rates of return of marginal projects in any sector;

(5) a risk or uncertainty premium;

(6) the rate of discount used in the private capital market to evaluate unequal time streams.

(The internal rate of return of a project is a particular discount rate value[142] at which the present value of its expected outputs equals that of the costs; i.e., the rate at which the computed net benefits are zero.) The search for an appropriate discount rate has generated endless academic discussion, which may be a reflection of its importance. The practical use of the discussion has been very little, however. Besides, it has probably come full circle, as witness Feldstein's[143] conclusion that "the interest rate even of a perfect capital market would be unsuitable for evaluating public investment projects." He recommends a social time preference rate "reflecting the Government's judgement of the relative social utility of consumption at different points in time."

Despite all the discussion, discount rates actually applied in valuing projects continue to range between 4 and 10 percent, the highest values usually being recommended for projects in less developed regions where living standards, some say, can only go up.

CHAPTER THREE

PROCESS OF PROJECT EVALUATION

A—INTRODUCTION

Project evaluation is a process of planning, monitoring and learning associated with the whole life cycle of a development project. It is also a frame of reference which relates an individual project as effectively as possible to a country's regional and overall development plan. This understanding is reflected in the proposed list of project-evaluation steps which has been developed by the Inter-Agency Working Group on Evaluation. Representing a systematic approach to asking questions at all phases of a project's evolution, the list of steps is designed for the requirements and possibilities of projects of virtually all sizes and degrees of complexity. It is based on four phases in the life cycle of project development as recognized by the Inter-Agency Study Group on Evaluation and agreed upon by the Administrative Committee on Co-ordination in its thirty-fourth report,[144] as follows: Phase I: Project preparation (identification of needs); Phase II: Appraisal of requests; Phase III: Operational control; and Phase IV: Assessment of results. However, while the Working Party's steps represent a general checklist of necessary questions within these four phases, this study goes further and presents the same four phases (and, with some modifications, essentially the same logic as implied in the Working Party's steps) in the form of a real-time network. A flow plan of this network is attached in an annex to this chapter. The flow plan is thought to be applicable to virtually any type of project, provided the proper judgement and selectivity leads to the necessary modification according to size and nature. Figure 16 represents a brief sketch of this approach.

FIGURE 16

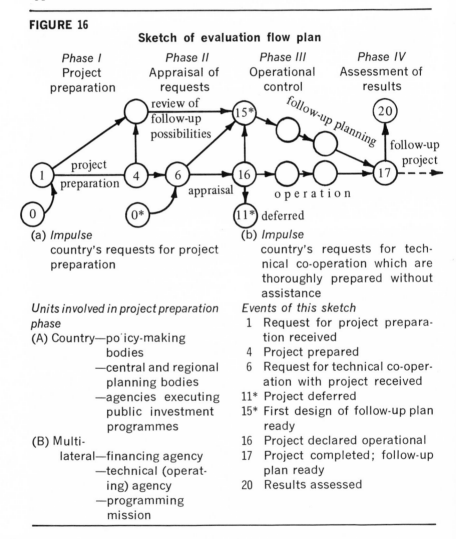

Sketch of evaluation flow plan

Phase I	Phase II	Phase III	Phase IV
Project preparation	Appraisal of requests	Operational control	Assessment of results

(a) *Impulse*
country's requests for project preparation

(b) *Impulse*
country's requests for technical co-operation which are thoroughly prepared without assistance

Units involved in project preparation phase
(A) Country—po icy-making
        bodies
    —central and regional
        planning bodies
    —agencies executing
        public investment
        programmes
(B) Multi-
    lateral—financing agency
    —technical (operat-
        ing) agency
    —programming
        mission

Events of this sketch
1   Request for project prepara-
        tion received
4   Project prepared
6   Request for technical co-oper-
        ation with project received
11* Project deferred
15* First design of follow-up plan
        ready
16 Project declared operational
17 Project completed; follow-up
        plan ready
20 Results assessed

The process of project evaluation is understood to be a continuously functioning monitoring mechanism, sequentially interrelated and adapted to the life cycle and nature of a particular project. Developing countries which already have sufficiently sophisticated development plans and mechanisms of project preparation at their disposal will enter the cycle at the appraisal phase (II). The first phase, project preparation, is indeed thought to be a mechanism which would serve countries with less planning experience and success, at their request, and which can be set up with various degrees of elaboration, cost and time, as necessary. Similarly, phase III: operational control, as well as the problem of follow-up planning (as suggested in the table above), should be understood as a flexible device. The specific designs of both aspects depend on the individual project and have to be specified accordingly. From the point of view of method, however, it is possible to show the logic and general approach from which such individual specifications can be derived.

The proposed flow plan is, like the Working Party's steps, understood to be an optimum constellation and, in this form, confined to the evaluation of individual projects. After being triggered by a country's request for project preparation, for example, it leads ideally in each phase to an optimally specified yet sufficiently flexible final event; i.e., phase I: a formal request for technical co-operation, technically and economically specified and designed within the framework of national and international priorities is ready for submission; phase II: the project, having gone through an economic, technical, financial and administrative appraisal process, and having been negotiated by the parties involved, is declared operational, or else is deferred; phase III: project operation and follow-up plan are completed and data are successively accumulated for operational control and assessment of results; phase IV: results are assessed, data stored for retrieval as necessary, follow-up project starts. The phases are further broken down into sets of consecutive functional segments which are necessary and sufficient constituents of each phase. For arriving at the still further detailed network, each segment is then broken down into its successively constituent activities and events.

One of the special features of the UNITAR approach to the evaluation problem is the examination and adaptation of management techniques to programme and project planning, including cost-benefit analysis, PERT network analysis, feedback for current management and operations and information retrieval for future programme planning.[145] The flow plan introduced in the annex to this chapter illustrates the utilization of such management techniques during the project's life cycle.[146]

B—Annotations to the Project Evaluation Flow Plan

While it is increasingly recognized that both skill and an effective organization of planning are main preconditions for accelerated economic and social development, it still remains true that a great number of developing countries are chronically deficient in their ability to programme and control development activities. Hence, a particular national Government may be explicitly aware of its general needs and may have formulated overall development objectives, but may require assistance in identifying those new development projects which should effectively contribute to a national development programme. In response to a request for assistance in project preparation, a multipartite programming mission of interdisciplinary experts can be set up, attention being particularly given to financial and follow-up requirements.

The task of the programming mission would be of a survey and analysis nature, with the specific purpose of assisting the particular national Government in formulating a subsequent request for multilateral technical co-operation in one of the development projects which the mission would identify. Such a subsequent request would be based on a draft work-plan prepared by the programming mission.

The flow plan proposes the division of the project-preparation phase (phase I) into two successive segments: (1) analysis of the framework of national development which constitutes the general environment of new development projects (segment 1), and (2) the specific analysis and related preparatory work in connexion with the subsequent request for technical co-operation with such projects (segment 2).

The programming mission will first be confronted with the analytical task of establishing the relationship of individual projects and aggregates of projects to the development plan and strategy. One aspect of this task may consist of putting foreseen new development activities into a comprehensive frame of reference, including the country's total external aid needs and resources. Furthermore, analysis of the development plan (or the closest existing substitute) with its long-term and intermediate-term objectives, as well as analysis of the actual state and future prospects of development (including evaluation of on-going and recently completed projects), should provide the qualitative and quantitative information base necessary for systematic identification of new development projects.

Secondly, given a systematically identified set of new candidate projects, multilateral assistance should be determined in the context of all actually and prospectively available resources, including national, bilateral, multilateral and non-governmental. Recalling the continuity of the evaluation process, it is assumed that a data storage and retrieval system, permitting the use of data on past experience (feed-back), would at this point greatly facilitate the mission's task and render its analysis operationally more useful

Following the analysis of the national framework, it is proposed that a series of considerations enter into the preparation process for individual projects, including preparatory technical design as well as economic, operational and other analyses (especially the exploration of follow-up possibilities). Operational analysis, specifically, includes an examination of such necessary pre-conditions as the country's ability to make effective use of the project results (absorptive capacity) and to provide the counterpart contribution. It also includes the multilateral agencies' ability to recruit international experts, procure equipment, and provide for sub-contracting arrangements (delivery capacity), etc. On the substantive side, built-in indicators for measuring performance and results and, in general, a thorough examination of the project's uncertainties on the demand as well as the supply side should be included in this preparatory analysis. Systematic examination of pos-sible alternative project designs as well as analysis and re-tooling of possible project designs drafted by the country's Government should lead to the formulation of a realistic draft plan of work and a request for multilateral technical co-operation. In addition, the programming mission should identify data and other counterpart requirements where the country can already initiate further preparation without prejudice to the subsequent appraisal of the request.

Project design and planning depends on the availability of qualita-tive and quantitative data about resources and about economic and social conditions in the project's environment. The specific statistical data which are needed depend, of course, on the type of project which is being prepared. The usefulness of available data, on the other hand, depends on accuracy, form, timeliness, scope and related criteria. For some projects the question may arise whether the available data, although to some degree inadequate, are sufficient for initiating de-tailed planning and implementation, or whether the project should be deferred until improved data are available. That is to say, while the relative importance of both statistical and non-statistical information will vary according to nature and objectives of the project under preparation, it will be up to the programming mission to decide whether additional data collection and research on a larger scale should be recommended (within the on-going preparatory process or with a separate project), whether specialized personnel should be called in to generate improved information on certain matters (e.g., the organiza-tion of base-line data, preparation of a workable set of qualitative and quantitative economic and social indicators about the project's effects in its given sector as well as other sectors which it is likely to affect) or whether the use of the existing information can be considered sufficient as an approximation.

To a large degree, a decision on such a question will depend on the costs and time involved, i.e., the economics of acquiring and using information of imperfect reliability. Indeed, the need for meaningful measurement of the risks associated with imperfect project-information systems becomes increasingly critical, the more complex the structure of a project plan. Both project preparation (phase I) and appraisal of requests (phase II) can be usefully described as processes of acquiring, measuring and communicating information to decision-makers. To perform these functions, analysis must be based on the close relationship between information and decision-making, and the "information system" represented by the project-preparation and appraisal phases should be subject to the same type of cost-benefit analysis as the project proper.

Submission of the prepared request by the national Government to the financing agency will trigger the process of appraisal (phase II).[147] The flow plan proposes again a division into two successive segments: (1) the process of multi-organizational analysis (segment 1); and (2) the submission of an appraisal report to the responsible body for decision, as well as the process of detail and final planning (segment 2).

The request and the draft plan of work should then be dispatched to the organizations directly involved in the requested project operation, including the technical (operating) agency for recommendations to the technical and operational questions and the agency designated for the follow-up function, for review of follow-up possibilities and for recommendations and planning proposals in terms of specific follow-up projects. The financing agency would be concerned with examining the economic, administrative and financial, legislative and other criteria.

Having received recommendations and data on all aspects, the financing agency will be in a position to prepare a detailed appraisal report about the project on the basis of established criteria.[148] Additional information may be required, which can be requested from the national Government. The completed appraisal report can then be submitted to the responsible body for approval or deferral.

Detailed planning of approved projects should include the whole organization of the project, its successive stages (segments 1, 2, 3, . . ., n), base-line data and targets, timely scheduling of personnel, equipment and other inputs and timely mobilization of counterpart financial, personnel and other contributions. The latter would presumably involve also the final negotiation of the plan of operations. In addition, at the same time the proper project-management information and communication system for timely monitoring and operational control should be set up. Depending on the delay between completion of the final plan of work and the actual beginning of operations in the field, a further review may be necessary before the project can be declared operational.

The effectiveness of a project can be understood as the degree to which it meets the demands of its targets and its environment—a variable which should be measured continuously during the process of operational control (built-in indicators). The final event of each segment of the project operation (1, 2, 3, . . ., n) represents a target which is planned to be met at a given time and at a given cost. Uncertainties, however, will require periodic reviews, adjustment of schedules and up-dating of the plan of work in the light of current performance problems and other unpredicted developments. The degree of effectiveness of operational control (phase III) can thus be expressed by its capability of timely prediction of such problems.

A first review of operations should take place at an early stage, with subsequent periodic reviews according to the logic of the project that is expressed by its division into successive segments. While planning of the follow-up project should begin simultaneously with the project operation, mutual adjustment between project operation and follow-up plan should be included in the phase of operational control. Furthermore, an additional control item may arise from the experience that targets and project objective can or must be modified eventually, as the accumulation of current operational information may lead to new recommendations.

Thus, viable operational control also implies an effective data storage and retrieval system at the individual project level which, moreover, serves the purpose of accumulating current project and environmental data for the final assessment of results (phase IV).

Completion of the project should include completion of the follow-up plan, together with its proper mechanisms for operational control. Apart from the immediate importance for the follow-up project, systematic assessment of results (undertaken on a multipartite basis) serves essentially two purposes and should be planned accordingly: (1) the accumulation of information relevant to the national development programme, and (2) the building up of the technical memory of the financing and technical (operating) agencies to the perusal of future preparatory, appraisal and operational control processes (feedback).

Note that the proposed phasing is not of a discrete nature, although it may be graphically suggested. On the contrary, emphasis throughout the study has been on continuity in the whole life cycle of a project; hence, the division of this cycle into phases is merely a device for analysis, planning and control. Parts of phases can overlap with preceding or succeeding phases to the degree called for by the nature of a particular project. For example, phases I and II are in fact interlocked by activity 5-10 (preparation of project data and other matters by the country). The assumption is made that at event 4 (request formulated, data requirements specified), it may already be fairly certain that a requested project will eventually be approved. Thus, the country may proceed to a certain degree with its preparations, under the assumption of approval. Also, the "borderline" of phases II and III is more or less arbitrary; but there is little analytical use in discussing at length the precise start of phase III. Event 16 (project declared operational) is the respective point in time chosen in the flow plan, because it is assumed to be the moment at which field operations actually start. However, pre-project planning (activities 11-13-14-15 in phase III) and operational control (re-planning and adjustment during implementation of segments 1, 2, 3, . . .,n in phase III) are parts of one continuous planning and control operation which covers both phases II and III. Finally, phase IV (assessment of results) is already a part of phase II to the extent to which current project and environmental data are accumulated for the purpose of assessment of the whole operation at its completion.

(c) ANNEX: PROCESS OF PROJECT EVALUATION (FLOW PLAN)

A. SUMMARY

Title	Including
Phase I: PROJECT PREPARATION	
Segment 1 Analysis of development plan, state of development and need for international assistance	—identification of objectives and priorities of development plan; evaluation of country's actual development programme; identification of new candidate projects
	—determination of UN system's assistance in the context of all available sources of aid
Segment 2 Preparation of individual project work plan and request	—preparatory technical, economic, operational and related analyses including follow-up possibilities (cost-benefit analysis)
	—formulation of draft work plan and request
Phase II: APPRAISAL OF REQUEST	
Segment 1 Analysis of request	—examination of technical economic and social, legisla-

Title	Including
Segment 2 Appraisal of request and planning of actual operation	tive administrative and financial, operational and follow-up aspects —appraisal report on the basis of analysis and established criteria —approval; deferral —preparation of final work plan and mechanism for operational control (PERT network analysis)

Phase III: OPERATIONAL CONTROL

Segments 1, 2, 3, . . ., n Implementation of segments 1, 2, 3, . . ., n of project; planning of follow-up project	—periodic review of operation, up-dating and adjustment of plan, including mutual adjustment with follow-up plan (PERT network analysis)

Phase IV: ASSESSMENT OF RESULTS

	—final examination and conclusion about direct and indirect results, including operational performance for the benefit of both the specific follow-up project and further activities in general —preparation of final work plan and mechanism for operational control of follow-up project

(b) List of Activities, Events and Responsibilities to Flow Plan

Events	Activities	Responsibility
Phase I: PROJECT PREPARATION		
Segment 1 Analysis		
0—Request for project preparation received		country
1—Request for project preparation		financing agency
	1–2 Appointment of Programming Mission	multipartite
2—Programming Mission appointed		Programming Mission
	2–3 Analysis of development plan, actual development and need for assistance in light of the country's objectives and priorities; identification of new projects	Programming Mission
3—Need for UN system's assistance determined		
Segment 2 Preparation of Individual Project Request		
	3–4 Analysis of candidate project: preparatory examination of technical, economic, financial, operational and follow-up possibilities; identification of data requirements; design and analysis of draft-work plan	Programming Mission
4—Request formulated; data requirements specified		
	5–10 Preparation of project data and other matters	Programming Mission
5—Request ready for submission		country
0*—Request ready for submission		country

Phase II: APPRAISAL OF REQUEST
Segment 1 Analysis of Request

Event	Activity	Agency
6—Request received	5-6 Submission of request	country
7—Request for analysis	6-9 Analysis of administrative, financial, economic, legislative and similar criteria	financing agency, follow-up agency, technical (operating) agency, financing agency
8—Request for analysis	7-9 Analysis and recommendations in terms of follow-up	follow-up agency
	8-9 Technical analysis and recommendations, including operational feasibility	technical (operating) agency
9—Analyses completed, recommendations received	9-10 Request for additional data to country	financing agency
	9-11 Completion of appraisal report	financing agency, technical (operating) agency
11—Appraisal report complete; (a) Approval, or: (b) Deferral [11*]	12-14 Detailed planning, PERT network analysis, including mechanisms for operational control	financing agency, financing agency
14—Planning complete	14-15 Final review and adjustment of project before inception	technical (operating) agency
	15-15*First design of follow-up plan	technical (operating) agency, follow-up agency

Events	Activities	Responsibility
Phase III: OPERATIONAL CONTROL		
Segment 1, 2, 3, . . . , n		
16—Project declared operational; beginning of operations		
	16-17 *Segment 1*—first review of operations; up-dating and adjustment of work plan	technical (operating) agency
	Segments 2, 3, . . . , n—periodic reviews, monitoring and adjustment, including questions related to follow-up project	
	15*-18 *Segments 1, 2, 3, . . . , n*—periodic and mutual adjustment of follow-up plan with on-going operation	follow-up agency
17—Project completed		technical (operating) agency
18—Follow-up plan completed, including mechanism for operational control		follow-up agency
Phase IV: ASSESSMENT OF RESULTS		
20—Results assessed, data stored for eventual retrieval	20*-21 Final follow-up planning; review of follow-up project before inception	multipartite
		follow-up agency
21—Follow-up project declared operational		follow-up agency

(c) Process of Project Evaluation: Flow Plan by Responsibilities

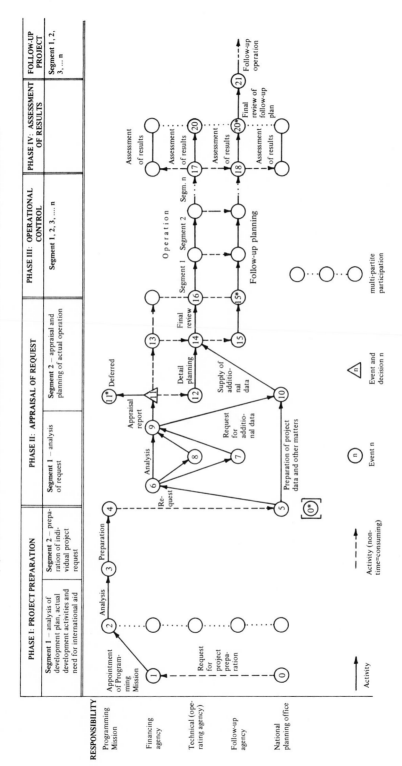

CONCLUDING REMARKS

In the light of some of the difficulties inherent in the application of PERT and cost-benefit analysis to the appraisal of development projects, it is appropriate to ask what these techniques are expected to do, and what they do not do.

To answer the first question, these techniques require the project designer to consider alternative methods of implementation. They make him examine all known or foreseeable factors of both input and output, together with their interrelationships through time. They put questions to him that require answers, if answers can be found. Otherwise, an estimate of "uncertainty" is at least determined for the consideration of the decision-makers.

On the other hand, these techniques do not make decisions. Yet they do provide an information base and an analytical frame to aid the decision-maker. The underlying expectation is that the greater the amount of relevant information that can be assembled and analysed for use in decision-making, the greater the chances of avoiding the wrong decisions.

It is clear also that rigorous application of the discipline may not always be possible or even relevant in given cases; however, the project designer at least has the option regarding how far to go. Often, a PERT plan even without the subsequent computations of "slack time" and "critical path" for the control mechanism would yield sufficient results.

Still other problems and inadequacies of technique have already been discussed or at least hinted at in various parts of the study. Nevertheless some additional insistence is called for regarding the caution necessary for the proper use of the suggested techniques.

In recapitulating, the starting point of this study is the "project" as a practically useful unit for the analysis of the variety of technical co-operation and other activity in the whole area of development. In principle, all such activity is subject to analysis (of varying usefulness) in terms of inputs in an *ad hoc* or already existing operational environment in which outputs are produced in identifiable periods of time. In this context some of the key problems stand out. For example, there is the issue of "measurement" and therefore of "quantification," since the value of the outputs units have to be composed with the value of the inputs. There is also the problem of measuring the contribution or the technical performance of the operational structure which forms the framework of the analysis of the project. An additional confounding factor for this quantification is "time" in its influence on the form of input and output flows and of the patterns of their changes over time. For practical reasons the exercise could not be another attempt at proposing primarily mathematical solutions, for even where these solutions are shown, the question of their particular application to a given project would still often remain insoluble. The study of the planning and programming of development therefore raises major problems of measurement and quantification. What use is the so-called unit or measure (and in money values), which is obtained on forcing factors like trainee-time in seminar, class or on-the-job instruction, or expert man-hours, or the expected effects of a new co-operative, into a single money unit quantification scheme? Are the gains for analysis worth the costs in sensitivity of the measure for the phenomena being measured, and worse, are the results of the analysis valid? The first question seeks a cost-benefit analysis on cost-benefit analysis itself, and is akin to the second in the context of all such problems whose resolution is bound to fail given Goedels Incompleteness Theorem, which postulates the impossibility of showing the validity of a logical system solely from within itself.

An attempt was made above to show that a valuation of "benefit" or "output" or "effect" is always analytically implicit from the link-up of inputs (from the project budget) and the projected, actual or resultant objectives and targets, to identified criteria specifications and tolerances; at the same time we recognise that the meaning or general proof of the validity of any such particular imputation is a problem, which so far remains unsolved.

Given the concept of "project," then, the first problem is to decide how best to go about implementing it. And this is where cost-benefit analysis linked with PERT network analysis come in as suggested approaches to the initial decision of whether a project should be selected at all, and if so, what alternative methods of implementation exist. Subsequently, PERT is also suggested as a useful implementation and control tool for feedback in revisions to an on-going project.

Laying out the PERT network forces the detailed examination of the usually numerous aspects of the project which necessarily interlock through time. Breaking down the project into its separate component parts enables the project designer to "see" the project as a whole. One could say that this should make "PERT-thinking" about projects valuable in itself, even though it might be considered unnecessary or impossible to utilize the complete analytical technique.

The crucial dependence of PERT analysis on activity times estimation and its practical handling of the uncertainty problem do approach development problems through their virtually universally constraining variable of time. However, this dependence also raises problems with the PERT approach itself, and demands the understanding that PERT is not necessarily the optimal solution of the problem of development projects. For any one of these projects, human and material resources (or their money values) needed, production methods and the performance of the resulting man-material-technique combinations are important considerations which are not always adequately handled by considering merely their effects on estimates of activity times of the PERT network. The alternative approach would be project analyses, for example, primarily in terms of the resource inputs needed for the project, or again in terms of the technical performance of the project implementation system.

In the link-up with cost-benefit analysis, however, an important use of the PERT network is in the identification problem; that is, ideally the research for a fool-proof answer to the crucial question of "what costs and what benefits?" Unfortunately, the real-time nature of the network quite often provides in practice merely a partial answer on the benefits side, inasmuch as it deals for any given segment with direct project effects or benefits. This is nevertheless a practical if partial "solution," and the techniques are after all no more than suggestive information aids to, but never substitutes for, decision-making by responsible authority.

FOOTNOTES

1. These views are summarized in the second report of the *Ad Hoc* Committee of Experts to Examine the Finances of the United Nations and the Specialized Agencies. In para. 77 of the report (doc. A/6343) the Committee commented, "With the needs of Member States in the area of economic and social development practically unlimited, and with limited available resources to meet these needs, it was all the more necessary to improve the effectiveness of the operations of the organizations so that the maximum return would be obtained from each unit of money expended. One way to help achieve this objective was to devise efficient techniques and guidelines for evaluating operations in order to identify and eliminate unproductive practices and activities which result in less than maximum organizational effectiveness and which do not meet the needs of Member States. The Committee believed that insufficient attention had been given to the establishment of common evaluation techniques and guidelines which could be applied by the United Nations family of organizations."

2. Official Records of the General Assembly, 16th session, Suppl. No. 17, p. 17.

3. Official records of the General Assembly, 21st session, Suppl. No. 3, pp. 4-6. While the latest average figure for the Decade is 4.8 percent, this obscures the difference between some rapidly developing countries and the many less fortunate countries. Furthermore, the average ignores the impact of population growth. If this were taken into account, the per capita growth in Latin America is less than 2 percent, in Africa 1 percent and in South Asia about ½ of one percent. (Speech of President MacNamara before the annual meeting of the World Bank, 30 Sept. 1968).

4. *Ibid.,* p. 6.

5. Official Records of the General Assembly, 22nd session, Second Committee Meeting No. 1166, p. 320, para. 7.

6. Official Records of the General Assembly, 21st session, Suppl. No. 16, res. 2218B **(XXI)**.

7. Doc. DP/L. 57, para. 28.

8. Official Records of the Economic and Social Council, 45th session, Suppl. No. 7, p. 25.

9. Official Records of the Economic and Social Council, 45th session, Suppl. No. 6, para. 119.

10. *Ibid.,* para. 127.

11. Official Records of the Economic and Social Council, 9th session, Suppl. No. 1, res. 222. **(IX)**.

12. *Ibid.*, para. 6(a).
13. Official Records of the Economic and Social Council. 37th session, Suppl. No. 1, res. 1042 (XXXVII).
14. Doc. A/6343, para. 74.
15. A subsidiary group of the Administrative Committee on Co-ordination. Doc. E/4486/Add. 1, annex VII, p. 2.
16. Co-ordination/R. 714.
17. The ACC requested UNITAR and UNDP to prepare a glossary of terms related to the ones already agreed upon in consultation with the United Nations and the Specialized Agencies and relevant ACC machinery. (E/4486/Add. 1, annex VII, para. 8). An informal working party of the Study Group elaborated additional definitions for consideration of the Group at its 1969 session. These were approved with minor modifications by the Study Group at its fifth session and were subsequently approved for use by the ACC at its 47th session, 28-29 April 1969.
18. See Glossary of Terms below.
19. Official Records of the Economic and Social Council, 36th session, Suppl. No. 1, res. 991 (XXXVI).
20. Official Records of the Economic and Social Council, 28th session, Suppl. No. 5, p. 77.
21. Official Records of the Economic and Social Council, 39th session, Suppl. No. 5. p. 94.
22. Doc. E/4151, para. 39.
23. Doc. DP/L. 67, p. 46.
24. *Regional Project of Kosovo-Metohija*, OECD, Paris (1968), p. 52.
25. *Draft Programme and Budget, 1967-68,* UNESCO 14 C/5, Introduction, paras. 168-9; underlining in original text.
26. *Approved Programme and Budget, 1967-68,* UNESCO 14 C/5 (res. 3.02).
27. Doc. E/4141/Add. 1, para. 99.
28. Doc. E/4501, derived from table on p. 4.
29. It should be noted that the regular programmes of the United Nations agencies are not in all cases strictly parallel in content or application with the UNDP technical assistance component. They are all oriented to problems of economic and social development broadly conceived but with limited differences arising from such factors as eligibility of countries to receive assistance, methods of implementation, project components and the substantive competence of the agency as set out in its basic terms of reference and subsequent resolutions. Agency programmes are briefly described in a report to the 6th session of the Governing Council, doc. DP/L. 72.
30. Associated assistance consists of expenditures from bilateral and other sources for Special Fund projects. These contributions, amounting to $126 million so far during the life of the Special Fund, do not appear in the financial accounts.
31. Associate experts are provided without cost by several European Governments to the agencies for assignment to developing countries. Experts on a payments basis are wholly financed by the receiving countries on a funds-in-trust basis but recruited and administered by the United Nations agency.
32. Doc. DP/L. 81, para. 6.
33. See doc. DP/L.67/Add. 4. Particulars of "associated assistance" are given project by project. It is estimated that in 1967, this assistance amounted to $26 million distributed among 166 projects in 60 countries.
34. A number of special purpose classifications exist, some designed to expose programme content. An example is the ACC classification used for

reporting to ECOSOC on expenditures of the United Nations system in relation to programmes. The latest report is contained in doc. E/4501.
35. An acceptable starting point in the consideration of a more informative
classification for sector/sub-sector analysis is shown in a newly published
table by UNDP contained in *The United Nations Development Programme
—A Note on the Range and Results of its Activities*, Sept. 1968 (no sym-
bol). This classification covers Special Fund and technical assistance activities. It provides some 30-odd sub-sectors distributed among the nine major
sectors generally used so far in published tabulations. It represents a substantial improvement. It is to be considered whether the new classification in its
present form can satisfactorily encompass some of the development activities
of other United Nations agencies so that a complete and organized picture
of total activity is available. This is a matter for further study.
A classification referring to technical assistance projects in the Expanded
Programme, prepared in 1965, is contained in Annex III of *15 Years and
150,000 Skills*, a publication of the former Technical Assistance Board
(Sales No. 65.I.18) This shows field expenditures from 1955 to 1964 by
nine major groups and 50 sub-groups. While it was not designed to include
Special Fund projects or those of non-UNDP agencies, it may be considered
as a useful working document in any study of the classification problem.
36. Doc. DP/L. 67, p. 54.
37. See note on the sample at the end of this section.
38. The value figures refer to the cost of experts only, and omit the cost of
fellowships and equipment.
39. Based on work-sheets especially provided by the UNDP.
40. See table V below.
41. All data compiled from DP/TA/L.5.
42. The regions of the Americas and Asia and the Far East were selected
for study. The shares of the programme devoted to activities in the four
categories set out in table VI are very similar to those of the other regions
in the United Nations classification, varying only by a few percentage points.
43. Some suggested economic and social indicators are set out at the end
of this section. The United Nations Research Institute for Social Development has established a data bank of about 100 social and economic indicators covering 115 countries with a population of one million or more for the
year 1960. These data are stored for computer retrieval. For particulars,
see *Research Notes, No. 1*, UNRISD, Geneva (1968), pp. 1-7.
44. The objectives of the groups are as follows: (a) to enable the recipient
country and the several aid-giving governments and institutions interested in
assisting that country jointly to consider its development programme and
needs in comprehensive, continuing fashion, rather than piecemeal, on the
basis of competent, objective information and analysis; (b) to facilitate the
provision of external finance, technical assistance and advice from appropriate sources, and their efficient channelling to meet priority needs; (c) to
make it easier to adjust the character and terms of aid to the country's
special circumstances; (d) to reduce confusion and disparity of criteria and
terms of aid from various sources, and duplication of effort in the presentation and review of programmes and projects; (e) to provide opportunities
for mitigating the problems associated with aid-tying and suppliers' credits;
and (f) to help to highlight deficiencies or difficulties in the country's economic performance and to influence or assist the taking of remedial actions.
(The World Bank, IDA and IFC, Policies and Operations, Washington,
1968, p. 72).
45. *Development Assistance Efforts and Policies*, OECD, Paris (1967),
p. 134.

46. This is essentially the theme of Guy Hunter's book, *The Best of Both Worlds*, London, Oxford University Press (1967).
47. I. M. D. Little, *Aid to Africa*, London, Pergamon Press (1964), p. 62.
48. *Ibid.*, pp 63, 64.
49. DP/SF/Reports, Series A. No. 35, Nov. 1968.
50. This point is taken up in a progress report on evaluation by the Administrator of UNDP (Doc. DP/L. 68, para. 13).
51. Guy Hunter makes this general point in *Manpower, Employment and Education in the Rural Economy of Tanzania* in saying, "Manpower policy should therefore be concerned with the right balance and structure of educational expenditure in relation to economic opportunity; it deals both with those who initiate opportunity and with those who can use it; it is the bridge between economic activity and educative effort." UNESCO International Institute for Educational Planning, Paris (1966), p. 12.
52. 15 years and 150,000 Skills, *op. cit.*, p. 1, p. 138.
53. Thirty-fourth Report of the Administrative Committee on Co-ordination, doc. E/4486, pp. 42-43.
54. Official Records of the Economic and Social Council, 45th session, Suppl. 6A, para. 331.
55. Official Records of the Economic and Social Council, 45th session, Suppl. No. 1, res. 1365.
56. Operative para. 1 of res. 1365.
57. Doc. DP/L.57, para. 26.
58. *Ibid.*, paras. 23-28.
59. Doc. E/AC.54/L.28, p. 9.
60. Some experience has been gained on a regional level by the Inter-American Committee on the Alliance for Progress (CIAP). This activity so far has not come up to initial expectations. See Raul S. Saez, "The nine wise men and the alliance for progress," *International Organization* (Winter 1968), pp. 244-269.
61. It is interesting to note that many of the formal project submissions at the January 1969 session of the Governing Council provided for reviews at mid-term or at a stated time period from inception. Indications in the project submissions showed that projects accounting for some 60 percent of the total earmarkings of $96 million were scheduled for review; projects representing 51 percent of total earmarkings were to be reviewed jointly by UNDP and the agencies concerned.
*By "period" is meant annual figures for, say, five years or more, depending upon the national statistics available.
62. Albert Waterston, *Development Planning, Lessons of Experience*, Baltimore, Johns Hopkins Press (1965), p. 61.
63. *Ibid.*, p. 65.
64. *Ibid.*, chaps. VIII and IX.
65. Official Records of the Economic and Social Council, 43rd session, Suppl. No. 7, pp. 13-19.
66. Suggestions for statistics related to development are contained in Statistical Series for the Use of Less Developed Countries in Programmes of Economic and Social Development, United Nations Publication—ST/STAT/Ser.M/31. The United Nations Research Institute for Social Development has prepared a list of indicators for a large number of countries. These data are especially selected to refer principally to the social aspects of development, but they include also relevant economic statistics.
67. Doc. E/AC.54/L.27, p. 11.
68. *Ibid.*, pp. 36-37.

69. Official Records of the Economic and Social Council, 43rd session, Suppl. No. 7, p. 25.
70. Doc. E/AC.54/SR. 14-19, p. 106.
71. Official Records of the Economic and Social Council, 39th session, Suppl. No. 1, res. 1079.
72. Official Records of the Economic and Social Council, 41st session, Suppl. No. 1, res. 1148.
73. Official Records of the Economic and Social Council, 43rd session, Suppl. No. 1, res. 1259.
74. Official Records of the Economic and Social Council, 26th session, Suppl. No. 1, res. 700.
75. *Ibid.,* res. 692.
76. Doc. E/4191, para. 75.
77. Doc. E/4312, Annex, para. 22.
78. I. M. D. Little and J. M. Clifford. *International Aid,* Chicago, Aldine (1966), p. 46.
79. John Kenneth Galbraith, *Economic Development,* Cambridge, Harvard University Press (1964), p. 58.
80. Official Records of the Economic and Social Council, 4th year, 9th session, Suppl. No. 1, res. 222 (IX).
81. Official Records of the Economic and Social Council, 18th session, Suppl. No. 1, res. 542 (XVIII).
82. *Ibid.,* para. 1 (vi).
83. Official Records of the Economic and Social Council, 30th session, Suppl. No. 1, res. 786 (XXX). Project budgeting permitted authorization of projects for four years, although the initial recommendation of TAB was for six years.
84. In doc. E/TAC/97.
85. Official Records of the Economic and Social Council, 32nd session, Suppl. No. 1, res. 854 (XXXII).
86. The percentages quoted above became, in the 1968 programme, 24.5, 21.3, 14.4, 16.7, 10.4 and 4.2. These shares represented 91.5 percent of the total UNDP/TA programme, the balance being distributed among the newer agencies.
87. Official Records of the Economic and Social Council, 43rd session, Suppl. No. 6.A, annex IV.
88. Official Records of the Economic and Social Council, 45th session, Suppl. No. 6, para. 47. This report also contains a discussion of the criteria used to establish and revise targets, paras. 49-59.
89. Official Records of the Economic and Social Council, 43rd session, Suppl. No. 6.A, paras. 35-39, 45th session, Suppl. No. 6, paras. 64-95 and 145-156.
90. The universal character of UNDP programmes is shown by the fact that in 1967, 91 countries and territories participated in Special Fund activities and 130 participated in technical assistance projects.
91. There are obviously many dimensions of development. Paul G. Clark has enumerated what he calls "dis-aggregated indicators of performance." These include: increase in GNP in constant prices; increase in agricultural production; increase in electricity production in response both to rising incomes and to extending urbanization and industrialization; share of gross investment in GNP—noted as the least reliable; domestic tax revenues as a share of total government expenditure; increase in quantity of exports; number of post-primary students per thousand population. (Quoted from Raymond F. Mikesell, *The Economics of Foreign Aid,* Chicago, Aldine (1968), p. 161). While most of these may be considered to have some relevance, the

list as a whole largely ignores social indicators and indicators referring to the development of the infrastructure which in most developing countries is basic to substantial progress.
92. Official Records of the Economic and Social Council, 45th session, Suppl. No. 6, para. 94.
93. The general appraisal of technical assistance projects is made in the light of UNDP resources available to the country (the "target"), the legislated criteria of UNDP, the immediate objectives of the project in relation to ultimate economic and social goals, the relationship of the project to past and present UNDP projects, the general political, economic and social context (including related activities in the country and its region) and the evaluation of comparable projects, current and previous, in the countries.
94. Doc. DP/L. 57, para. 31.
95. *Ibid.*
96. *Ibid.*, para. 15.
97. Doc. DP/L. 79, para. 8.
98. United Nations Development Programme, *Definitive Proposals for Revising the Special Fund Reporting System,* New York (January 1969), p. 4.
99. "Comments on Methods for Reporting and Evaluating Progress under Plan Implementation" (paper presented by M. F. Millikan, member of the Committee for Development Planning), in *Planning and Plan Implementation,* United Nations Publication, Sales No. 67.II.B.14.
100. For a more detailed though non-technical introduction to this thinking, see S. Beer, *Management Science, "The Business Use of Operations Research,"* New York, Doubleday (1968).
101. CPM was developed by M. R. Walker of DuPont and J. E. Kelly of Remington Rand, in 1957. PERT was first described in D. G. Malcolm et al., "Applications of a Technique for R and D Program Evaluation," *Operations Research,* 1959, pp. 646-669.
102. See C. MacMillan and R. F. Gonzales *Systems Analysis. A Computer Approach to Decision Models,* Homewood, Irwin (1965), pp. 189-210; S. B. Richmond, *Operations Research for Management Decisions,* New York, Ronald Press (1968), pp. 481-498.
103. This section is concerned with the essence of the PERT technique. Computer applications and PERT/Cost Analysis are not treated separately.
104. Information on the subject which is not relevant to this illustration is not included. The time considerations introduced below are not related to the actual project. The example is chosen for illustration purposes only; it has *no* operational significance.
105. This citation and the information leading to the subsequent brief description of the project is taken from the relevant Governing Council document.
106. In an administrative environment, this hierarchical technique of networking was recently used for setting up the new Ministry of Land and Natural Resources in the United Kingdom. See W. S. Ryan, "Network Analysis in Forming a New Organization," C.A.S. Occasional Paper No. 3, London (1967).
107. Some authors distinguish the Critical Path Method (CPM) from the Programme Evaluation and Review Technique (PERT) by emphasizing that, whereas CPM attempts to *determine* the expected times of completion of a total project and its component sub-projects, PERT goes further and estimates the *statistical variances* associated with these expected times of completion. This distinction is here referred to by the following two sections on "Critical Path under Certainty" and "Uncertain Time Estimates."
108. Richmond, *op. cit.,* p. 487.

109. E.g., persons assigned with the responsibility of estimating time may have had little or no experience with the particular type of work involved in a given activity.

110. There is agreement that this concept is valid in theory; what seems not clear is how it should be computed in cases with discontinuity in the frequency-distribution curve—cases which ·are common in real life. A start is made, with *simulation,* in creating an artificial model of the behaviour of the system described by the network: a time is taken at random from the distribution of each event 1, 2, 3, . . ., n, and the effects are evaluated. Then another set will be chosen, and so forth. In this way the behaviour of the whole network is simulated, and if this exercise is done sufficiently often and at sufficient speed, information on the entire range of possible behaviour of the network becomes available. Cf. S. Beer, *Decision and Control,* New York, Wiley (1966), pp. 172-180.

111. Beside the paper by Malcolm et al., *op. cit.,* the following references are used for this section: McMillan, Gonzales, *op. cit.;* R. I. Levin, C. A. Kirkpatrick, *Planning and Control with PERT/CPM,* New York, McGraw Hill (1966); Richmond, *op. cit.*

112. The qualification of specialists providing time estimates must include thorough understanding of the work to be done. Moreover, the PERT team must plan and activate procedures for actually obtaining the required information. Only with continuous information flows is it possible to predict the time at which each event in the project is likely to occur.

113. An actual PERT exercise should develop explicit definitions for these three types of estimates requested. Moreover, the specialist estimating elapsed-time values of an activity should not estimate succeeding and preceding activities, nor should he know these values. If this rule is followed, the system will acquire a self-correcting tendency, the larger the number of estimated activities in the network.

114. Malcolm et al., *op. cit.*

115. A modification though not a fundamental change is proposed in a recent paper by J. J. Moder and E. G. Rodgers, "Judgment Estimates of the Moments of PERT Type Distributions," *Management Science,* Oct. 1968, pp.B 76-83. The argument in that paper, however, is not directly relevant for this introductory presentation.

116. A mathematical development of this procedure is given in Richmond, *op. cit.,* pp. 488-491.

117. This is justified since the variance of the sum of n random variables is equal to the sum of the variances. However, the distribution of the portion of the network with the smaller expectation, but not necessarily with the smaller distribution, is assumed away (see table XI), the variance of event 56 is in fact larger than the variance of event 58. On possible effects resulting from this phenomenon, see A. R. Klingel, "Bias in PERT Project Completion Time Calculations for a Real Network," *Management Science,* Dec. 1966, pp.B 194-201.

118. Cf. W. T. Morris, *Management Science, A Bayesian Introduction,* Englewood Cliffs, Prentice Hall (1968), pp. 5-8, et passim. "Institutionalized" of course implies the customary model simplification of one coherent and rational organization which is faced with a decision problem that must be conceptualized (e.g., "a machine has broken down," "someone has resigned," etc.). It may be argued that the structure of management directly and indirectly involved in the operation and control of a development project is far more complex and, moreover, cannot be understood only on grounds of rationality. However, the basic logic of the learning model remains the same. The more heterogeneous the constituents of an organization, the more diffuse its purposes, objectives and performance. This situation of course

is precisely what is calling for a more urgent consideration of the management control and learning issue. See also H. L. Wilensky, *Organizational Intelligence: Knowledge and Policy in Industry and Government*, New York, Basic Books (1967), p. 39.

119. P. Y. Tiberghien; T. Rovière, "Application de la méthode PERT au projet ESSOR," *Energie Nucléaire*, juin 1965.

120. It is suggested that monthly up-dating provides the means for examining those activities that are currently most critical; the whole project network should be evaluated quarterly; reporting cycles for various sub-projects and other components should be staggered according to the major up-dating schedule (cf. PERT, "A Dynamic Project Planning and Control Method," White Plains, IBM Data Processing Application [no year], p. 22). Ultimately it depends, of course, on the particular project what type of a reporting cycle should be adopted.

121. "More specifically, at the point which maximizes the probability of its being met within the slack interval." For the statistical relationship involved in this statement, see PERT, "A Dynamic Project Planning and Control Method," *op. cit.*, pp. 19, 24.

122. A three-stage amplifier can be illustrated as follows: "A traveller just misses a bus and has to wait two hours for the next causing him to just miss a train and incur a six-hour delay; this causes him to miss his airplane and incur a two-day delay." Cf. Beer, *Management Science, op. cit.*, p. 77.

123. See P. Masse, *Le plan ou l'anti-hasard*. Paris, Gallimard (1965), pp. 188-244.

124. E.g., W. Meissner, "The Theory of Dynamic Programming and Problems of Development Planning," *Konjunkturpolitik*, March 1966, pp. 31-57.

125. For a general theory of the decision–learning approach, see W. J. Morris, *op. cit.*, pp. 151-168.

126. See for example R. D. Archibald and R. L. Villoria. *Network Based Management Systems*, New York, Wiley (1967); PERT, "A Dynamic Project Planning and Control Method," *op. cit.*; D. L. Cook, *Program Evaluation and Review Technique: Applications in Education*, Washington, D.C., U.S. Dept. of Health, Education and Welfare (1966); and many others.

127. M. K. Starr, *Product Design and Decision Theory*, Englewood Cliffs, Prentice Hall (1963), pp. 2 ff.

128. This is reflected by the multiplicity of post-PERT management and control techniques which are at present on the market, e.g., CPS, PEP, LESS, TOPS, CRAM, SCANS, COMET, PROMPT ("Management and Control Techniques," U.S. Department of Commerce, Washington, 1963), GERT (A. A. B. Pritsker, and W. W. Happ, in *Journal for Industrial Engineering*, May 1966), MOST (A. L. Lannone, in *The Chartered Mechanical Engineer*, June 1967), etc.

129. S. E. Elmaghraby, "On Generalized Activity Networks," *The Journal of Industrial Engineering*, Dec. 1966, pp. 621 ff.

130. Malcolm et al., *op. cit.*, pp. 658-688; C. E. Law and D. C. Lach, "Implementing the Critical Path Method in a Large Organization," *Canadian Operations Research Journal*, Mar. 1966, pp. 35-47.

131. Cf. Law, Lach, *op. cit.*, p. 37; proposing a project of about 200 activities as "suitable" for the first formal test.

132. "Sufficient" may be considered a level of detail allowing to maintain control, but not too burdensome for all parties involved. A rule of thumb is proposed, stating that no activity should include more than 5 percent of the total anticipated cost and time of the project (*ibid.*, p. 39).

133. For a model of the PERT computerized data-processing cycle, see Malcolm et al., *op. cit.*, p. 663. An example of a computer programme is included in MacMillan and Gonzales, *op. cit.*, pp. 197-210.

134. R. Dorfman, "Basic Economic and Technologic Concepts," in A. Maass et al., *Design of Water Resource Systems*, London, Macmillan (1962), p. 90.
135. H. A. Thomas, "The Animal Farm a Mathematical Model for the Discussion of Social Standards for Control of the Environment," *Quarterly Journal of Economics*, vol. LXXVII, pp. 143-148.
136. *Ibid.*, pp. 145-146.
137. A. R. Prest and R. Turvey, "Cost-benefit Analysis: A Survey," *Economic Journal*, December 1965, p. 731. N. Scott, "Some Problems of Cost-benefit Analysis," *UNRISD Report No. 7*, Geneva, 1966, pp. 33 ff.
138. Scott, *op. cit.*, p. 16.
139. *Ibid.*, p. 37.
140. Prest and Turvey, *op. cit.*, pp. 687 ff.
141. P. O. Steiner, "Choosing Among the Alternative Investments in the Water Resources Field," *American Economic Review*, vol. XLIX, Dec. 1959, p. 897.
142. This particular "r" value is the equivalent of Keynes' marginal efficiency of capital and is properly applicable to the outputs/"benefits" and inputs/ "costs" streams of the single investment project under analysis. Nevertheless, it is often confused with Irving Fisher's "rate of return over cost," whereas the latter properly applies to the comparison of at least two projects, envisaged by Keynes' ratio. The practical equivalent of both approaches are used at different phases of the approach to project evaluation envisaged in this paper. In the first phase, alternative implementation procedures for a project are compared. Fisher's rate of return over cost is then applicable, while subsequently, with a particular project implementation procedure approved, the internal rate of return would match the discounted benefits and costs streams within the chosen single project, like Keynes' marginal efficiency of capital. (See A. A. Alchian, "The Rate of Interest, Fisher's Rate of Return Over Costs and Keynes' Internal Rate of Return," *American Economic Review*, vol. XLV, Dec. 1955. pp. 938-943; and S. A. Marglin, *op. cit.*, pp. 47-67).
143. M. S. Feldstein, "The Social Time Preference Discount Rate in Cost Benefit Analysis," *The Economic Journal*, vol. LXXIV, June 1964, pp. 360-379.
144. "Development and Co-ordination of the Activities of the Organizations within the United Nations System," 34th report of ACC. Annex VII, "Evaluation of Programmes of Technical Co-operation," E/4486/Add.1, 19 April 1968.
145. "Evaluation of Technical Co-operation Programmes," Note by the Secretary-General, E/4508 (UNITAR/EX/13), 9 May 1968.
146. The issue of data storage and retrieval, i.e., the orderly and effective arrangements for information feedback and monitoring, is introduced as a concept within the process of project evaluation, but is not elaborated in detail.
147. Projects which are sufficiently prepared by the country's own planning mechanism and for which assistance is requested independently of the proposed preparatory phase will enter the evaluation process at this point.
148. Such a report may include information on (1) the background, (2) the specific sector in which the project should operate, (3) details of the project itself, (4) the *ex ante* evaluation (cost-benefit analysis) and recommendations. Reports of this type are an integrated part of the appraisal process at IRBD, serving the Loan Committee as an information base for its decisions on projects. The cost-benefit approach to *ex ante* evaluation is described in a separate part of this study.

INDEX

129

65-66, 111 (*fig.*)
in planning, 56-58
Gross domestic product, as indicator, 53

Health
  development plans and, 11, 44
  expenditures for
    distribution of, 36 (*table*)
    recurring, 42
    in study sample, 40 (*table*)
  government budget for, as indi-
    cator, 54
High Commission for Refugees
  (HCR), 25
Housing expenditures
  physical planning and, 36 (*table*)
  in study sample, 40 (*table*)

Imports of food, as indicator, 53
Indicators, social and economic,
  list of, 53-54
Industry, 44
  expenditures for
    distribution of, 36 (*table*)
    in study sample, 40 (*table*)
  regional development plans and, 11
Infant mortality, as indicator, 53
Information
  for programme development,
    41-43, 47-49, 105-7, 109
  for programme evaluation, 107-8
Institutional constraints on programme planning, 60-62
Integrated development programme,
  definition of, 22
Inter-Agency Study Group on
  Evaluation, 103, 105
Inter-Agency Working Group on
  Evaluation, 103, 105
International Bank for Recon-
  struction and Development,
  see World Bank
International Labour Conference,
  20
International Monetary Fund
  consultative groups and, 43
  expenditures of, 26
Inter-regional projects
  definition of, 22
  distribution of, by components,

38 (*table*)
distribution of experts in,
  37 (*table*)
Interest rates in cost-benefit
  analysis, 102-3
Iraq, 39

Jenny, Béat Alexander, 8
Joint programming, 50-51

Land policy, central importance
  of, 60-61
Latest allowable time, 86 (*table*)
Latin America, 54, 55-56
Leonard, William, 7-8
Literacy, as indicator, 53
Little, I.M.D., 44, 60
Longevity of projects, 28-33

Management control system, in net-
  work analysis, 89-92
Meteorology, regional plans and, 11
Millikan, Max F., 51
Mexico, 39
Monitoring of projects through net-
  work analysis, 89-92
Multi-sector projects, expenditures
  for
    distribution of, 36 (*table*)
    in study sample, 40 (*table*)

National priorities, conflicts with
  development plans of, 11
National projects of regional
  development, definition of, 22
Netherlands, 10
Network analysis, *see* PERT net-
  work analysis
Nigeria, 39
Nwali, Offia, 8

OECD, 20
  consortia organized by, 43
Operational control
  as aspect of evaluation, 13-15,
    103-5, 110
  definition of, 23
  events involved in, 114 (*fig.*)
  information and communication
    systems for, 108-9
  by network analysis, 89-92